THE COMPLETE
WATERCOLOR
ARTIST

THE COMPLETE
WATERCOLOR
ARTIST

JENNY RODWELL

This 1987 edition published by
Crescent Books, distributed by
Crown Publishers, Inc.,
225 Park Avenue South,
New York,
New York, 10003

First impression 1987
Text © 1987 by Jenny Rodwell

ISBN 0-517-63400-7

Typeset by Peter MacDonald, Twickenham
Origination by Union Grafica, Verona, Italy
Printed and bound in Italy by Poligrafici Calderara

Art Editor	Tony Paine
Project Editor	Sally MacEachern
Photography	Ian Howes
	Don Wood (Materials Section)
Artists	Ian Sidaway
	Richard Wise (cover illustration)
Designers	Grub Street Design, London
	Carol Suffling
Art Assistant	Sue Brinkhurst
Picture Researcher	Liz Eddisan
Art Director	Stephen McCurdy
Editorial Director	Jeremy Harwood
Publishing Director	Nigel Perryman

h g f e d c b a

Contents

6
INTRODUCTION

8
THE WATERCOLOR TRADITION

76
MATERIALS AND EQUIPMENT

104
PRACTICAL WATERCOLOR
TECHNIQUES AND PROJECTS

227
SIMPLE TECHNIQUES

250
GLOSSARY AND INDEX

INTRODUCTION

WATERCOLORS HAVE BEEN popular for centuries. Their luminous transparency helps to produce a freshness that cannot be equalled by any other medium. However, there are pitfalls as well. The attraction of watercolor has encouraged many people to work in it – and quite a few of these have been disappointed by the results. This is because they have plunged into the business of painting without the necessary initial understanding of the principles and techniques of the medium with which they are working. They may not have realized, for instance, that it is vital to be patient and allow the colors to dry, and so have ended up with paper awash with uncontrolled color. Or they may have become alarmed by the difficulty of obtaining flat washes.

The aim of this book is to provide the necessary grounding to help all artists working in watercolor to overcome such difficulties and so enable them to exploit the potential of the medium to the full. It is therefore not just a beginner's tool; it will help those who have already begun, and also those who have some experience, but who wish to broaden their methods and use of materials. With knowledge of the appropriate techniques and with practice, painting in watercolor can be one of the most exciting of all art forms. It can also satisfy two quite different methods of working – the methodical and the spontaneous.

The best approaches

With some knowledge of the basic materials and techniques, and with experimentation, all the characteristics of watercolors can be turned to advantage. For instance, you can adopt a strictly methodical approach to your painting, if you wish. You can make a fairly precise drawing, plan where your colors are to go, mix and dilute them to get the right shades, and then carefully block in the shapes and build up the tones, allowing the paint to dry between stages. You can also use "drybrush" technique, squeezing water off the brush for intricate, textured work.

On the other hand, the very fact that watercolors tend to flood and "bleed" into each other when wet means that a spontaneous approach can be adopted, too. This means that you can set out deliberately to let "chance" play an exciting part in the creation of your pictures. Both approaches, too, can sometimes be combined; a small amount of flow, or color-bleeding, can work well within the confines of a carefully structured picture.

Watercolor characteristics

What makes the medium seem daunting to the beginner is the fact that watercolors are transparent; this means that you cannot paint a light color over a dark one, because the darker color will show through. Once you have made a dark mark on the paper, you are committed, and you can alter the effect only by painting an even darker color on top of it. This is the chief difference between watercolors and oil paints. You cannot simply paint over a picture in layers, as you can with oils, literally covering up mistakes.

Other differences affect the way you can actually paint. With oils, for instance, the addition of the "highlights" – the lighter, sometimes pure white, tones that usually depict the reflections of light onto the objects in the picture – can sometimes be left until the final stages. With watercolors, however, the colors are conventionally applied from "light to dark". Therefore the highlights are often simply areas of the picture that have been left unpainted; the white is the paper itself. When colors are applied, the lighter tones go on first, and the darker ones are built up on top of this. This means that you need to know which areas of the picture are going to be the lighter ones, for they will be left with less paint or none at all.

Moreover, oils can be manipulated while they are being applied; the paint can be actually moved around on the surface of the canvas, and the colors will not adhere properly to the surface until they are dry. Watercolors, however, cannot be used in this way, since, as their name implies, they are mixed with water. It is usually water that governs the tone – the more diluted the color, the lighter the tone.

Mixed media

There have always been different types of watercolor, but nowadays the range is greater than ever before. And, of course, watercolor can be mixed with other media.

As you will see from the historical survey of the watercolor tradition that forms the opening section of this book, there have been times when watercolors were used to make preliminary sketches for oils – and also periods when it was considered "impure" to add any other materials to what was considered strictly a "watercolor painting". Today, however, many artists prefer to vary the use of their materials without inhibition. For instance, you can use colored pencils with watercolor washes, while pen and ink and gouache (an opaque version of watercolor) all have their possibilities. Opaque watercolor is older than might be supposed – many of the Old Masters used gouache, or "body color" as it was known, for the final highlights. Others used ink with watercolor washes.

Remember, though, that, although the medium has its disciplines and rules, you should never allow them to become a straitjacket and dominate you. What matters above all else is that you establish which methods, techniques and materials best suit you and your approach to your painting; if you bear this in mind as well as the necessary basic precepts, you will not go far wrong.

THE WATERCOLOR TRADITION

WATERCOLORS ARE ONE of the oldest artistic mediums known. Physical evidence of their use by Stone Age people still survives – hidden in the darkness of caves that, for reasons unknown, were decorated by the world's first artists. From this time onwards, watercolors added their own particular flavor to artistic history.

It was not until the 18th century, however, that watercolor paintings became recognized as works of art in their own right. Since then, they have enjoyed enduring popularity among amateur, as well as professional, artists. Two of their chief qualities are their freshness and versatility, which, as this section of the book demonstrates, have been constant factors in the development of the watercolor tradition from earliest times to the present day.

THE FORERUNNERS
PREHISTORIC ART

ALTHOUGH LITTLE IS KNOWN about our prehistoric ancestors of some 20,000 years ago, they certainly included some sophisticated artists. These figurative painters of the Old Stone Age, or Upper Paleolithic period, crawled into the inner recesses of huge limestone caverns, taking with them primitive paints made from earth, mineral and animal pigments – red and yellow ochre, manganese, graphite, and iron oxides of a deep blood red color – as well as tools for scratching outlines, implements for rubbing the paint onto the surface, and in some instances, tubes of bone for blowing or spraying very fine powdered pigments. Black marks found on cave walls and roofs indicate that they must have illuminated the awesome darkness with the faint light given by simple, animal fat lamps.

The artists would have found it no easy task to reach the roofs and walls of these deep galleries. It is thought that they adopted uncomfortable positions on the shoulders or backs of others, or lay flat on their backs on narrow ledges. The paints they used were made from pigment that had been pounded to powder, thinned with water and mixed with some kind of binding medium that clung to the rock surface. The moisturized make-up of these paints helped to preserve the paintings in the damp atmosphere of the limestone caves.

Working in this way, the painters created vivid and lifelike pictures, mostly of the animals – typically the bison – which Paleolithic people hunted. In some cases, the artists repeatedly painted new images over the top of their previous work. Many of these final paintings survived, undisturbed for thousands of years until comparatively modern times.

The first discovery of these spectacular paintings was made in the late 19th century at Altamira, northern Spain. They immediately challenged current ideas of the culture and abilities of prehistoric peoples. Many historians of the time were incredulous, unable to believe that "those creatures" were so technically skilled. Some condemned the cave paintings as fakes.

Another major discovery was made in 1940 when four boys playing near Montignac, in the Dordogne, France, came across the Lascaux Cave paintings. Since then other paintings have been found, and 20th century scholars, aided by scientific testing, have accepted the cave paintings as genuine. However, it was difficult for people to accept that the true forerunners of the revered Masters were these primitive Stone Age painters who decorated remote, dark caverns so many thousands of years ago.

STANDING BISON
Altamira, Spain

Here is vivid evidence of the ability of the cave painters – the heavy, rather menacing strength of the bison has been captured in masterful representational fashion. It is typical of the distinct detail with which many of the animals were painted, and shows levels of observation that seem surprisingly modern – quite unlike some of the symbolic and stylized methods found in much primitive and ancient art. In the cave paintings, the animal takes precedence. The human form is rarely seen, and then almost as a stick figure in cartoon form, sometimes pointing arrows at the animals.

Ever since the discovery of these cave paintings, there has been speculation about their purpose, and particularly about why they were painted in the dark. The suggestion that Stone Age people might have had keener eyesight seems unlikely, since it is almost certain that they had to light the caves. The most common theory is that the paintings were a form of magic, and that the darkness might have been intended to inspire religious awe as the shapes and colors flickered in the lamplight. The over-painting of one picture on top of another suggests that the artists were not painting to decorate the caves, but in the belief that the act of depicting an animal would help in the hunting of it.

EARLY MATERIALS
(Papyrus and Parchment)

THE PAINTERS WHO decorated buildings, tombs and papyrus texts throughout 3000 relatively stable years of ancient Egyptian history were not encouraged to be adventurous, neither were they recognized as artists in their own right. The work of writing and painting was done by the same craftsmen, the scribes, who were likely to have been trained in a broad range of skills. Yet there appears to have been a hierarchy among them, for some were major administrative figures in Egyptian government. It seems likely that a team of scribes was sent to carry out a specific task, some drawing outlines, some writing and some adding color and detail, perhaps with a "master" intervening at crucial points.

The painters worked with pigments which came mainly from minerals. Iron oxides, for instance, were used for red, while blue was made from silica, copper and calcium. Carbon produced black, and chalk, or gypsum, formed the basis of white. Other pigments included yellow ochre, and a green derived from powdered malachite. The pigments were diluted with water, and a binding agent, probably of vegetable or animal gum, was added to them. With these paints, and sometimes beginning with a thin overall color wash, the scribes produced some brilliant colors, many of which are still surprisingly intense. It is the mineral composition of the paints which has helped them to retain this vividness over the centuries. The equipment found in tombs is unexpectedly simple, forming a striking contrast with the sophisticated results achieved by the scribe-painters. Both writing and painting were done with brushes, ranging from fine rush brushes with chewed ends to pieces of palm-rib and fibrous wood beaten out into a stiff brush-shape at one end.

With this equipment, and after rigid training, a scribe painter was expected to create pictures according to a set style, known as "aspective". Figures were a formalized mixture of profile and frontal view – stylized eyes, drawn from the front, are combined with a head which is in profile; the legs are in profile, but the shoulders face squarely to the front; and so on. The rules were rarely broken. But there was scope for creativity as can be seen from the lively poses; the tricks of design where limbs or clothes cross boundary lines; the vivid animals, birds and plants represented; and, not least, from the mixing of colors on the palette which produced subtle secondary hues.

Papyrus formed the accepted surface for writing and painting during ancient times. The papyrus surface was made by splitting the stems of the papyrus reed, which grew in abundance in marshy areas. Later parchment, made from animal skins, gained ground in Greek and Roman times (although papyrus long remained the most favored), and gradually came into widespread use, providing the surfaces for Biblical texts and for the spectacularly illustrated religious scripts of the early centuries AD.

NAKHTE AND HIS WIFE
Book of the Dead (c. 1320-1290 BC)

Like the cave-painters thousands of years before them, many of the artists of ancient Egypt painted for "galleries" that would, they thought, remain in perpetual darkness. They created vivid colors and animated scenes on papyrus rolls, which were then sealed inside the tombs of great personages.

These texts were intended to assist their owners when they came before Osiris, the judge of the dead, and also to guide them through the intricate preparations for an afterlife. The papyrus rolls found by archeologists have been gathered together

and, although the versions differ, the collection is known as the Book of the Dead.

The version shown here is a papyrus manuscript prepared for Nakhte, a high-ranking scribe and military leader. He and his wife are shown emerging from their house to greet the rising sun and the god Osiris, who is sitting on a dais. Like many such scripts, the text itself is visually subordinate, done in plain black without elaboration, very much like a modern illustrated book. The illustration is linear, and yet complex: the figures are drawn in formal profile, but with typical Egyptian aspective, the trees around the pool appear to be growing at right angles. (LEFT)

PORTRAIT AND SYMBOL OF ST MATTHEW
Lindisfarne Gospels (c. AD 690-700)

The Lindisfarne Gospels, illustrated manuscripts from the remote monastery of Lindisfarne, on Holy Island, off the north-east English coast, represent an artistic triumph of the Anglo-Saxon era. This particular illustration is linear, without much feeling of depth, but it is enriched with the bright colors typical of the great age of manuscript illumination. (TOP)

THE FORERUNNERS
FRESCOES

WITH THE ART OF fresco painting, humankind can be said to have reached one of its peaks. Real fresco is the most beautiful form of decorating the interiors and exteriors of buildings yet produced by artists. Sadly, however, it is no longer in widespread use, as the techniques involved are not suited to modern construction methods. Fresco painting rose to its high point during the Renaissance, and it seems unlikely that any technique devised in the future will ever be so brilliantly attractive and, at the same time, so effective as a means of decorating walls and roofs. When carrying out classical or true fresco, known by its Italian name of *Fresco buono*, the artist applies pigments mixed with water directly onto wet plaster – the process involves plastering and painting in one meticulously coordinated operation. If the plaster has been made from absolutely pure materials – such as white lime which is free from gypsum, and pure sand – then the acids in the air cause a chemical reaction which crystallizes the pigments into the plaster. The result is an image which is actually part of the building itself, rather than a decoration added later.

The term *Fresco secco* is used for painting onto dry plaster. Before the artist begins painting, the wall is wetted thoroughly with lime water. Ancient Rome produced some beautiful wall paintings, most of which were probably painted onto plaster that had already dried.

It was *Fresco buono*, however, which came triumphantly into its own, from approximately the 13th century to the 16th – the work done then has been unmatched since. The most meticulous standards were reached: only the purest lime – two years at least in a lime pit – could be used; then the freshly-laid surface was painted with powdered earth pigments ground in purest water. The chapel frescoes done by Giotto (1266/7-1337) in Padua are recognized as masterpieces, as are his frescoes in the chapels of Santa Croce, Florence.

In the 16th century many painters reverted to *Fresco secco*. In the 19th century, there were attempts in northern Europe to revive pure fresco, but they were defeated by the dampness of the climate, which retained acids produced by smoke.

SISTINE CHAPEL CEILING
Michelangelo Buonarroti
(begun in 1508)

In one of the world's most famous
masterpieces, Michelangelo (1475-1564)
brought the whole ceiling of the Sistine
Chapel into brilliant life with figures that
seem to float and glide off the surface. This
is fresco at its grandest.

The series of paintings, based on
Genesis, took two and a half years to
complete, gradually creeping forward
across the great ceiling, section by section,
in time with the final laying of plaster.

In executing frescoes, especially major
ones of this sort, it was essential, first, to
create a complete guide, or cartoon, and this
had to clearly indicate each day's area of
painting. Most artists planned their color
schemes exactly, before the actual work
started. Sheets of tracing could then be
placed over the surface and the design
imprinted by indenting, or by powdering
through holes.

Meanwhile, the plaster brought to the
site was the product of years of careful
tending. The lime would be stored in a lime
pit and watered and stirred for at least two
years before being pure enough for use. Any
mistakes in the making of the plaster could
mean that the fresco would soon be distorted
by reactions of discoloring caused by
chemical impurities.

The plaster was applied in three layers.
The first layer, which was known as the
trusilar, was rough-cast, and this was
followed by a second layer, the arricciato,
which was richer in lime. Next, the area
which could be covered by the painter in one
day was estimated, and the third layer was
applied to that surface only. Known as the
intonaco, this was richer still in lime.

In the Sistine Chapel, plastering and
painting would have been executed from
high scaffolds. The painting itself was
initially built up in thin transparent
washes, which ran into the wet plaster and
were absorbed by it – a flooding technique
similar to a watercolor wash. At this stage,
more detail was added, including
highlights in the form of pure white lime.
The Italian painters were fond of using
hatching and shading for conveying shape
and form.

CHINESE ART

WATER-BASED PAINTS have been employed in China for at least 3000 years, with long and tenacious traditions of philosophy and religion often governing their use.

The art of both China and Japan is noted for its liveliness: the figures are obviously moving; the bamboos sway; leaves and flowers rock in the wind. The techniques which have produced these effects are based partly upon the fact that writing was done with a brush on silk or paper. The absorbent surfaces of these materials encouraged Chinese painters to use thin, non-viscous media, such as ink and water-soluble paints.

A silk-making industry, based on silkworm farming, had been established in China by 2000 BC. The silk obtained from the cocoon of the silkworm readily absorbs water and is ideal for painting in delicate washes. Painted silk was hung on walls as decoration, or kept in a scroll as a primitive form of book.

The Chinese also produced paper at an early date. It is said to have been invented in AD 105 by Tsai-Lun, who beat plants into fibers which he then wove into webbing. Not long afterwards, materials such as rags and old nets were also being used in paper-making.

For centuries, the art of painting in China was regarded as inseparable from that of writing. Far from being the preserve of specialist artists, it was considered an essential skill – particularly for scholars, poets, philosophers, and even emperors – and was taught from childhood. As a result, many pictures strongly reflect philosophical themes.

Some are aimed at imparting wisdom to the viewer in a fairly direct and conscious way, supported occasionally by beautifully-designed pieces of text. Other pictures, however, especially the great landscapes, are visual forms of meditation.

Their landscapes attempt to achieve a tranquil relationship with nature. Those figures which appear are often dwarfed by looming mountains and overhanging trees. Whirls of mist curl around the dramatically emphasized mountains. The humans appear small and fragile, reflecting their humble and transient place in the natural and irresistible order of the world. The ideas that formed the intellectual basis for these pictures came from doctrines such as Taoism and Buddhism which stressed the need to accept one's place in the grand scheme of nature.

Although, in China, landscape has always been considered the proper subject for paintings, people are portrayed from time to time as major and interesting characters. The human body, however, does not appear as the main focus of visual interest, as is so frequently the case in western art. Instead, the figures are seen as part of the process of daily life and ritual. One of the best known of these silk handscrolls, painted by the Emperor Hui Tsang (who reigned from 1101-25), depicted women preparing a scroll of newly-woven silk. Another well known artist, Chou Fang (c. 740-800), painted high-ranking ladies in graceful postures taken from daily life at court. They are posed beside sprigs of foliage, small animals, or birds which complement their fashionable elegance.

IRIS WITH BUTTERFLIES AND INSECTS
(16th century) by an anonymous artist

This handscroll in ink and colors on silk comes from a period that marks a resurgence of new freedom and color in Chinese art, during the Ming Dynasty (1368-1644).

Under the influence of such philosophical themes as Taoism and Buddhism, some Chinese painting had been going through a kind of purification, towards a very simple and austere ideal of tranquility. Mu-ch'i (c. 1200-1270), a Zen monk painter, produced a mystical picture entitled "The Evening Bell of a Temple in Fog", where distant, tiny points of landscape can just be glimpsed through the haze. The landscapes of other painters, too, became increasingly composed of empty space; some of them brilliantly capturing a mood of mystery and distance with a few strokes of ink.

After Mongol conquerors had ruled China between 1280 and 1368, the country became reunited under a native dynasty – the Ming. For the arts, there was a period of relaxation and revived color, accompanied by brighter pictures of animals and court scenes. Officially-appointed artists reappeared, but they were not subjected to quite such severe restrictions as before. Bird and flower painters, for example, once again worked for the court, but no longer under the discipline which had required close study of a subject. In some cases, this resulted in work which was merely decorative, or repetitious of earlier masters – but some painters, like the anonymous one featured here, benefited from the new freedoms. Imaginative touches resulted in beautiful pictures and raised the term "decorative" onto a higher plane.

THE ADMONITIONS OF THE INSTRUCTRESS TO THE COURT LADIES (detail)
(4th century) by Ku K'ai-chih

One of the greatest masters of early Chinese painting was at work during the period of the "six dynasties" when, from AD 222-589, the previous Han Empire was broken up into three kingdoms. Ku K'ai-chih (344-c.405) lived under the Eastern Chin dynasty. Already, strict guidelines had been laid down for paintings, including approved ways of using brushes, faithfulness to objects, and the copying of earlier works to maintain continuity of tradition. There are extant copies of Ku K'ai-chih's work, and this handscroll, in ink and colors on silk, is probably one of his original paintings.

The figures, outlined in fine brushstrokes, are clearly individual characters, rather than stylized human forms. The scroll has a serious moral theme, based on the often fragile relationships between men and women, but there is also a slightly irreverent, humorous touch.

Ku K'ai-chih's paintings, like much of Chinese art, were inspired by literary and philosophical ideas. This scroll illustrates some writings by Chang Hua. The moral tone is demonstrated by a piece of text which says, "Men all know how to adorn their faces but none know how to ornament their minds".

RADHA AND KRISHNA IN A GROVE
from the Rajasthani school (18th century)

A god, who has descended to human form, and a milkmaid, wander through an idyllic grove in this love scene from one of the most colorful periods of Indian art – the Rajput-Hindu tradition of miniature painting. This tradition flourished between the 16th and 19th centuries, in two main schools – the Rajasthani in Rajputana, and the Pahari in the Punjab. It had its roots in court life and entertainment, and drew much of its inspiration from Indian epics and legends.

The cult of Vishnu was extremely popular throughout northern India, inspiring plays, stories, songs and pictures. The Hindu god Vishnu took human form in

various ways, including the role of Krishna, who represents joy and love – the antidotes to suffering. There is a lightly mischievous side to him and his amorous adventures with the cowmaidens, among whom Radha was his favorite, had a great fascination for Indian storytellers and artists, who often concentrated on this happier aspect of an old cult, which in earlier, sterner versions had told of Krishna leaving his maidens and fighting against tyranny.

Flowers and jewellery are painted with precision, and the faces are in profile, stylized in a way which was common in this tradition. The overall concern for design and color and the stylized hills and buildings, give a magical quality to the picture. It escapes from mundane reality and takes the viewer to a happier world.

THE FIRST WATERCOLOR ARTIST
ALBRECHT DÜRER
(1471-1528)

ALBRECHT DÜRER was the first European painter to use watercolor as a serious alternative to oils. His love of natural history and his careful observation of plants, birds and animals led him into a full exploration of the medium. For watercolor, with its delicate, transparent tones, made it possible for him to achieve scientific precision in his depiction of nature. Dürer trained both as an engraver and as an oil painter; a combination which enabled him to use line and color to produce watercolors which are striking in their detail.

Yet, after Dürer's death, despite the virtuosity of his pictures, watercolor fell back into obscurity – regarded as a secondary medium suitable for miniatures, decorating manuscripts, and as a working-step towards oils. Nearly 300 years were to pass before it gained recognition as a medium in its own right.

The turn of the 15th century is generally considered to mark the end of the Early, and the beginning of the High, Renaissance. Dürer, therefore, lived through some of the most important decades in the history of art. He was a contemporary of artistic giants – including Michelangelo, Raphael, Titian, Botticelli, Hieronymus Bosch and Leonardo Da Vinci.

The young Dürer learned engraving from his father, who was a goldsmith, and he later became especially skilled in copperplate engravings. From an early age, he had thus developed a highly sensitive awareness of line with its varying thickness and its depiction of detail. This approach is reflected in all his watercolors, particularly his botanical works, which are a combination of transparent color and beautifully observed outlines.

His mastery of color was further developed when he became a pupil in a painter's studio. Later, in the 1490s, he travelled through Germany and visited Italy. Biographers note that he saw the work of other artists, and was impressed by it; he also began to paint landscapes in watercolors. Back in his native city of Nuremberg, Dürer opened his own studio in 1495. Later, he sought and won patronage from some of the most powerful figures of his time, including Charles V, and the Holy Roman Emperor, Maximilian I. Meanwhile, Nuremberg was becoming one of the first strongholds of Protestantism. Dürer favored the doctrines of the Reformation and became a friend of Luther's. A true Renaissance man, his wide range of interests also led him to write treatises on geometry, perspective and fortifications.

THE GREAT PIECE OF TURF
(1503) by Albrecht Dürer

This picture is a classic example of the cliché, "before its time". Dürer's watercolor of a section of grass and wild flowers stood apart from the mainstream art of its time and remained isolated for centuries. Its style of stark realism uncannily anticipates much modern painting and illustration.

In order to show every plant in its entirety, Dürer took almost a ground-level, cross-section view, rather than setting up a conventional visual composition. At the same time, he exploited the transparency of watercolor – using it to depict shape and form, and to capture the feeling of sunlight on the foliage.

Dürer was blissfully untroubled by a convention which would have a dominating effect on watercolorists in later centuries, particularly in the 18th century – in order to be "pure", a watercolor painting had to be truly transparent; therefore, the use of opaque white body color was considered to be "cheating". In this picture, he used body color to sculpt the forms of the foliage; while some of the outlines of the grass and leaves were drawn in pen and ink. The color was blocked in initially, with fairly loose brushstrokes. Then, he worked into areas of the picture until each blade of grass showed up crisply and separately from its environment.

A GUIDE FOR OTHER MEDIA
RUBENS
(1577-1640)

To a 20th century observer, Rubens' great studio in Antwerp would have resembled a bustling, well-organized factory. The Flemish master created nearly 1,000 pictures during his lifetime, many of them enormous panels which would span the entire wall of a modern house. Watercolor was a key process in the production of these massive oil paintings.

Peter Paul Rubens (1577-1640) was able to produce such an astonishing output as a result of the methods he devised for executing paintings. First he decided upon the basic outlines of each picture. Next, he made a drawing, and from this he created a detailed watercolor sketch. The use of watercolor enabled Rubens to quickly work out the arrangement of color and tone before committing the painting to oils. The sketch acted as a design for the workshop. Rubens' assistants enlarged it to its full scale and filled in the main areas. Rubens then added the finishing touches.

Throughout most of the 16th and 17th centuries, the use of watercolor in Europe was restricted to the secondary role of acting as a tone and color guide for oil paintings. It was, in fact, a natural extension of the cartoon.

A cartoon, in this sense, is a full-scale drawing for an oil painting, or a fresco. It was pinned to a wall, canvas or panel and then transferred to the surface, either by tracing over the outlines, or by pricking small holes along them, so that fine charcoal dust could be sifted through.

Initially, cartoons were drawings done in monochrome, but artists increasingly used white body color for the highlights. This application of bright white enabled them to work out the full tonal range of the picture at cartoon stage. When Raphael (1483-1520) was commissioned to produce designs for tapestries which were to hang in the Sistine Chapel, he produced full-scale colored cartoons, using a type of watercolor.

Anthony van Dyck (1599-1641) also used watercolor as a working stage for oil paintings, but in a very different way from Rubens. Van Dyck built up a store of possible backgrounds for his portraits by painting watercolor sketches, often of landscapes, from life. The sketches acted as color guides, and formed the basis for the realistic backdrops in his pictures.

After Rubens' death, many of his assistants perpetuated the tradition of using watercolor as a preparatory stage in oil painting. Jacob Jordaens (1593-1678), for instance, finished some of the master's uncompleted works, and then for the rest of his career he continued to follow Rubens' techniques closely.

Apart from Dürer, who had had died in the first half of the 16th century, there were no major painters using watercolor as an end in itself. There was, however, one slight exception. The preliminary watercolor sketches of a few artists in the Netherlands started to gain recognition as paintings in their own right. The most important of these artists were the van Ostade brothers – Adriaen (1610-84) and Isaack (1621-49) – and Allart van Everdingen (1621-75), whose work influenced many Dutch contemporaries.

NEREID AND TRITON
by Peter Paul Rubens

Nereid, a mythical nymph of the Aegean Sea, and Triton, the legendary son of the god Poseidon, are depicted here in a dramatic picture which establishes a harmony between the shapes of the figures and the movement of the waves. Nereid is a typically Rubenesque voluptuous woman; while Triton is shown with the shell horn traditionally borne by this character who was supposedly half human and half dolphin.

On top of these rich forms and colors, Rubens has used pure opaque white; and in this case the white body color is employed not only to describe highlights but also to emphasize the shiny wetness of the subject.

RAPHAEL

(The Sistine Chapel Tapestries)

IN THE SECOND decade of the 16th century, a series of giant watercolors was transported across Europe from Italy to Brussels. Raphael (1483-1520) had been commissioned to design a set of 10 vast tapestries to adorn the Sistine Chapel, which was being refurbished. Although the Italians were acknowledged masters of painting, the Flemish were considered to be better at manufacturing tapestries. Raphael, therefore, painted 10 watercolor cartoons, some of them standing more than nine feet (three meters) high, to act as a guide for the weavers.

Although some of their colors have faded, eight of these cartoons have survived – a fact which surprises historians since the cartoons were painted on sheets of paper which had been joined together. In addition, no great care was taken to preserve them after the tapestries had been completed. It was only in later years that they came to be regarded as precious artworks.

Raphael's experience as an engraver was to prove invaluable when he had to tackle one of the major problems involved in designing the tapestries: the weavers would not be standing in front of their work, but would weave from behind the tapestry frame. This meant that Raphael had to paint the watercolors as mirror images. Christ, for example, is shown lifting his left hand, instead of his right. This "reverse style" is a standard technique of engraving, where the image on the metal plate produces a reverse imprint on paper.

Raphael knew that his cartoons would be used by weavers hundreds of miles away, with no possibility of consultation, and that therefore it was important to make the designs clear and simple. This desire for simplicity governed every aspect of the cartoons. Each color used in the figures was chosen, so that it is dramatically lighter, or darker, than the color behind it. The colors selected for the clothing are pure and vivid; the folds and creases of the material depicted in stark contrast. The facial expressions are bold, even exaggerated, thus making their interpretation even more uncomplicated. Raphael's designs were also intended to smooth the transition from paint to silks: the silks of the tapestry would be less manageable, and color subtleties difficult to translate.

The watercolors were full-sized cartoons enabling the weavers to work from them directly. At that time, it would have been difficult to manufacture a suitable surface large enough for this purpose; therefore, Raphael painted onto sheets of paper which had been glued together. The pigments were bound in animal glue, which made the colors opaque; some of them have faded with time. Raphael's assistants would have ground and mixed these colors.

The studio would have found it easy to divide the labor for these watercolor cartoons. The assistants would have blocked in wide areas of color, which would dry quickly, allowing for further stages. The master himself would have filled in the more intricate details, such as facial expressions.

TAPESTRY OF THE MIRACULOUS DRAFT OF FISHES
(1515-16) by Raphael

The weavers have done their job to perfection, but they were restricted by the nature of tapestry itself. The colors, the gestures and the facial expressions have all been translated faithfully into the tapestry silk. The stark contrast between colors has helped enormously, as can be seen, for instance, from the way the figures and birds stand out vividly against the background.

The texture of tapestry means that it inevitably flattens the images in a picture. It is difficult, if not impossible, to create the illusion of reality, as the viewer is all too aware of looking at a flat design – the weave itself is a constant reminder of this. For instance, the atmospheric perspective, which in the painting pushes the hills back into the distance, has not been successfully interpreted in the tapestry, although the colors are accurately depicted. The clear edges of the hills mean that the haziness of far distance has been lost.

THE MONOCHROME TRADITION
TONAL WASHES

A BROWN WASH, used extensively in the 17th century as a preliminary tonal sketch, gradually became increasingly accepted as a finished art form in its own right. It was this neutral medium, rather than any range of brighter colors, which anticipated the great watercolor tradition of the 18th century. A few artists introduced a limited number of colors into their range of washes, but these were earthy and subdued, and were never used to interpret actual colors in a realistic way. Instead, they were seen as an extension of tone and not as colors in themselves. Earth reds, siennas and umbers were usually employed to establish the tones of a subsequent oil painting, when the realistic colors would be painted in, with the help of this tonal guide.

A rapid wash is a versatile technique, which enables artists to work out their ideas quickly in a way that is not possible with massive, traditional oil paintings. It is, therefore, easy to understand why some of these washes began to develop into finished work, and to gain respect as a independent part of an artist's repertoire. Many washes intended purely as preliminary guides for oils have a strikingly complete quality about them, so rich are their variations in tone. In fact, looking back at the work of Rembrandt and also at that of Nicolas Poussin (1594-1665), it is often impossible to differentiate between a wash sketch that was intended as a guide, and one which was a finished work. Some scenes were interpreted in loose strokes and blobs of color, and are surprisingly modern in appearance. This is particularly true of some of the washes done by Rembrandt (1606-69), and the French painter Claude Lorraine (1600-82), whose wash drawings were loose and free compared with his oils.

Brown wash was a true forerunner of watercolor, in that painters could use it to build up a picture with layer upon layer of thin tone. Extremely dark tones could be achieved by using this method. Often the light paper color was used to depict the light tones and highlights – a technique that would be exploited during the classic age of watercolor painting.

However, artists often used monochrome washes outdoors to make quick sketches of landscapes, and this required a different technique. The artist would choose a gray, or medium-toned paper – often white or off-white, tinted with a light color wash – to establish a middle tone. The artist could then work towards darker, or lighter tones by applying brown wash – usually sepia or bister – for the shadows, and opaque body color for the highlights. The darker initial surface meant that the outdoor artist could establish a middle tone quickly, instead of gradually breaking down an expanse of flat white.

THE GOOD SAMARITAN ARRIVING AT THE INN
(1641-43) by Rembrandt

This loose sketch of a famous Biblical scene was done in pen and brush, and brown ink, corrected in places with opaque white. The group of figures with the horse have been drawn with a pen, but peripheral shapes have been drawn directly with a brush as the artist laid down the washes. In fact, many of Rembrandt's most beautiful drawings were done with the brush alone.

One of the most distinctive characteristics of Rembrandt's oil paintings is his personal way of interpreting light. It is not always technically accurate; for instance, his light may come from different sources, or he may have added some "extra" light-source in order to emphasize a particular feature. His success with this unconventional approach is a tribute to his exceptional ability. In the hands of a lesser painter the results would undoubtedly appear artificial, or staged. Rembrandt used light and shade for effect, and to create a sense of drama, rather than in any realistic way.

In this picture, by working with brush in areas outside the central group, the artist has been able to suggest distance and the amorphous shapes of night. The shadows, where the central light has diffused outwards, have been painted in diluted sepia, thus creating an eerie night-time light.

FATHER OF ENGLISH WATERCOLOR
PAUL SANDBY
(1725-1809)

IT IS FITTING that Paul Sandby should be regarded as the "father of English watercolor", for he was a lively, experimental painter who was able to break free of his own training and traditions. The work of this former military draftsman marks the beginning of the great period of English watercolor painting, when it changed from being a dry topographical recording medium to a fresh means of interpreting nature.

In the years immediately following the 1745 rebellion of Bonnie Prince Charlie, Sandby was sent to Scotland to work on a military survey. As he followed in the footsteps of the redcoats, he visited some of the wildest parts of the Highlands, and although his task was to record the lie of the land in strictly practical charts, he developed a love of scenery that was to emerge later in his painting.

Sandby was totally fascinated by nature, both in its calm and mature state, as in Windsor Great Park, and in its bleak and rugged regions. Sandby lived in London from about 1752, and he often painted in Windsor Park, where his brother was Deputy Ranger. Thomas Sandby (1721-98) had produced tinted sketches of guns and equipment for the army, as well as some architectural drawings, and he went on to paint pictures which were very similar to Paul's.

Despite his technical background, Paul Sandby introduced a style which reflects an emotional response to the landscape, and is one of the main characteristics of his work. Sandby was highly sensitive to atmosphere and to light. He applied brushstrokes loosely in order to suggest the falling of sunlight on foliage, climatic variations, the wildness of remote areas, and the feeling evoked by glimpses of crumbling medieval walls in ancient parkland.

Sandby was also very innovative and imaginative in his use of materials. He was said, for example, to have once mixed a "warm" black color by combining the burnt edges of his breakfast croissant with gum water. Sandby felt under no obligation to adhere to a strictly transparent way of working, and therefore he freely applied both watercolor and body color, either in combination, or separately.

In 1760, Sandby exhibited a series of pictures in London. This was the first public display of watercolors as pictures in their own right, rather than "tinted drawings". From then on, Sandby had a profound influence on the watercolor artists of his day. This influence was increased by the fact that he was very much a public figure, who took an active role in artistic events, and was a founder member of the Royal Academy, London.

A MILKMAID IN WINDSOR GREAT PARK
(1765-70) by Paul Sandby

In creating this composition, dominated by the tall, twisting trunks of the central trees, Sandby has produced what came to be regarded as the classic watercolor. The transparency of the medium has been brilliantly exploited to produce a sense of delicate light, and cool shade. He has used very pale washes in the middle and far distance to give the impression of hazy sunlight, while the long shadows on the woodland floor introduce the concept of time passing.

Sandby was more interested in creating a general impression of foliage, than in a detailed rendering of each individual leaf or twig. He has achieved this effect with loose brushstrokes; producing bursts of reflected sunlight around the tops of the trees, and allowing a pale golden wash to show through the leaf canopy.

The shadowy areas of the overhanging branches have been built up with freely applied patches of warm and cool neutral tones. The forms of the trunks and foliage have been brushed in loosely and sketchily, and the shadows on the trunks suggest the gnarled and ancient texture of the bark. This loose brushwork was a fresh and totally innovative approach to painting an historic subject, such as Windsor Castle.

THE ENGLISH WATERCOLOR PAINTERS
J. M. W. TURNER
(1775-1851)

TURNER IS UNIVERSALLY acknowledged as one of the true masters of watercolor, even though he spent much of his life trying to escape from this medium into what he saw as the grander world of oils. He held his first watercolor exhibition at the astonishingly early age of 15, and went on to push the possibilities of the medium to the limits of innovation.

In his watercolors, Turner strove to capture the very essence of light – so much so that some of his pictures seem almost to dissolve as you look at them. Even more remarkably, he succeeded in achieving the same effect in the heavier and less spontaneous medium of oil paint, though not everyone approved. Critics in the 19th century said that Turner's landscapes were "pictures of nothing".

Criticism was something that Turner met throughout his artistic career; eventually it was to turn him into a sour and withdrawn man, openly contemptuous of public taste. His artistic life started when he became an apprentice. After coloring prints for a beer merchant, he started work at 13 for the topographer Thomas Malton, making detailed maps, plans and drawings. This apprenticeship taught Turner a great deal about the importance of precision and perspective and much of his early work was clearly influenced by this kind of detail.

The young Turner was also helped by a typical 18th century "enthusiast". This was Dr. Monro, who founded an informal art school to encourage young artists of the day, including Turner and a contemporary who greatly influenced him, Thomas Girtin (*see pp 34-5*).

Up to the age of 21, Turner was essentially a watercolorist and, throughout his life, he continued to paint in the medium, as he found he could make money from this type of work, which he partly based on his many sketching tours. His travels took him to Italy several times, which was where he became fascinated by color, especially when related to light. This obsession came to dominate his work; it also excited furious controversy. When you look at his pictures, including the large oil paintings which he increasingly undertook, you can see this obsession literally bursting into the images, and distorting convention as a result.

Turner's oil paintings were bitterly attacked, though by the 1840s they were also being strongly defended. Some critics said that his oils were "enlarged watercolors"; although this is incorrect, the two naturally influenced each other. He left 20,000 watercolors behind him on his death; few of them had ever been exhibited to the public, but they are now highly praised for the light and color effects.

TINTERN ABBEY
(1794) by J.M.W. Turner

This picture shows the heavy influence of Turner's topographic apprenticeship, with its intricate attention to line and structure. But there are already signs of change. Although the basic drawing and underlying structure remain crucial, tone is described in areas of warm and cool wash, which Turner uses not just to describe form, but also to create atmosphere.

As Turner progressed, the subdued grays, blues and sepias of his early palette gave way to a more colorful approach. The lines faded, becoming less intense as the artist became increasingly involved with light, space and color.

THE ENGLISH WATERCOLOR PAINTERS
MONRO'S ACADEMY

DR. THOMAS MONRO (1759-1833) was a man ahead of his times. A medical doctor, he specialized in mental illness – a field which, at that time, was often the target for contempt and mockery. Monro was also an amateur artist and a collector of art. In 1794, this interest in art and artists inspired him to open his own "school" for young watercolor painters, at his home in Adelphi Terrace, London.

After buying easels, drawing boards and materials, Monro made it known that he would provide supper and half a crown to anyone who attended for a few hours. The young artists who gathered at Monro's home to copy the works of other painters were brought into contact with some of the eminent artists of the day. At that time artists were apprenticed, rather than sent to art school, and the idea of forums and central workplaces was a new one; the Royal Academy had been started only in 1768, and the Society of Artists in 1760.

Watercolor painting probably owes more to this doctor of medicine than to any of the artistic personalities of the time; for Monro's school brought together the two greatest watercolor painters of the late 18th and early 19th century – J.M.W. Turner and Thomas Girtin.

Both Turner and Girtin worked as topographical draftsmen until, aged 19, they met at the Academy. As part of their early apprenticeship at Dr. Monro's school, they performed rigorous artistic exercises, including the meticulous copying of some of Canaletto's drawings which were part of Monro's collection. These exercises, a common form of tuition for apprentices at that time, helped to refine their topographical skills. The two young painters cooperated and influenced each other, to the extent that it is difficult to tell some of their earlier works apart.

After a visit to Paris, Girtin developed his craft to such a level that, despite the shortness of his life, he personifies an important stage in the evolution of watercolor painting. His work bridges the gap between the stained drawings of the 18th century and the fully-fledged medium of the 19th century. When Girtin died, aged 27, Turner expressed his admiration with the words, "If poor Tom had lived, I should have starved".

THE GARDEN TERRACE
by Thomas Girtin

This harmonious and tranquil picture demonstrates what an inventive watercolorist the artist was. Thomas Girtin (1775-1802) introduced among other things a fresh way of painting trees: he turned away from the linear representation of foliage, and instead executed leaf masses and clusters of trees with a series of broad washes, the dense areas of foliage being indicated by layers of darker tone.

In 1794 Girtin went on the first of his sketching tours. His color scheme broadened from a blue, green, gray theme which reflected Cozens' work, into more varied, rich, warm tones. Girtin loved the rolling hills and valleys of Yorkshire, but he also excelled at classical subjects and complicated townscapes. This picture reflects Girtin's mastery of structure and linear perspective, a technique which was lavishly demonstrated later in an enormous panoramic view of London exhibited in 1802, the year of his death.

A PORTRAIT OF DR. THOMAS MONRO
by Henry Monro.

Young painters were encouraged to gather at the Doctor's home to draw and paint. These gatherings gradually became known as the "Monro School", or "Monro Academy".

THE FIGURE

(Away from Landscape)

DURING THE 18TH century, watercolor painting was dominated by landscape – grand sweeps of Alpine scenery, romantic views of crumbling ruins, and the architecture of towns and villages. Artists had escaped from the tight topographical style of tinted drawings, and watercolor became a recognized medium in its own right.

The human figure often appeared, alone or in groups, in these landscape paintings, but rarely in a central role. Mostly, figures were represented sentimentally, in romantic settings designed to appeal to popular taste.

The work of painters such as James Ward (1769-1859) and Joshua Cristall (1767-1847) heralded a different approach. In their pictures, the figure was often central, while landscape became a background for the person. These painters were interested in figures, not as romantic characters, but as real people. Ward, in particular, avoided the romantic, and the "Frenchified" stylishness of 18th century taste. There is a sturdiness and honesty about his peasants and country people, who are painted in their working clothes, with every idiosyncrasy of dress and facial expression included.

Meanwhile, the caricature, which provides such brilliant insights into the 18th century's corruption, social pretensions and bawdiness, had evolved into an art form in its own right. The term "caricature" was first used in English in 1748, although the idea of exaggerating human characteristics was not new. These pictures – some done in bitter satire and some with affection – often involved the use of watercolor, if only to color drawings and engravings. One of the best-known 18th century caricaturists, Hogarth (1697-1764), used watercolor occasionally to add a color wash to drawings.

Other prominent caricaturists employed watercolor much more frequently, combining the mass-produced commercial picture with the skill of the watercolorist to produce a work of art. Thomas Rowlandson (1756-1827) and James Gillray (1757-1815) are regarded as two of the foremost exponents of this technique.

THE FRENCH HUNT
by Thomas Rowlandson

Rowlandson began work as a serious painter – often of portraits – but, having spent a fortune left to him by an aunt, he then paid off his debts with a prolific output of drawings. He was popular during his own lifetime, but after his death he was not to become popular again until the end of the 19th century.

Although the subject of this picture is robust, sometimes gross, the handling is not. The colors and tones are subtle, and the line never loses its sensitivity. Rowlandson was not an analyzer of society, nor an intellectual. Incidents and scenes, rather than social comment, appealed to him. He worked quickly; a few lines may depict an entire figure, while a face is sometimes drawn with the simplicity of caricature. In a group composition, such as this, the faces are drawn to a formula, rather than individually conceived. Rowlandson spent two years in Paris studying art, and it has been said that his use of line was more French than English. He certainly liked sinuous, winding shapes and billowing forms; sometimes, as in this case, they take on a more scrawny and scraggy appearance – usually they were painted in thin washes of local color.

Rowlandson's early work was strongly influenced by John Hamilton Mortimer (1740-79), a painter and draftsman. The hatchings and cross-hatchings, for instance, used to emphasize tone in Rowlandson's paintings are borrowed from Mortimer.

THE ENGLISH WATERCOLOR PAINTERS
A NEW TRADITION
(Figures and Fantasy)

A NEW TRADITION began to develop towards the end of the 18th century, led by a few highly imaginative painters. Their approach was in stark contrast to the strictly observed, realistic and representational pictures of people and landscapes that had so far typified the 18th century watercolorists. The new subjects were drawn from the imagination; from ideas that soared above what some might regard as mundane. It was a visionary approach, removed from the idea that artists should paint the world as they saw it.

William Blake (1757-1827), was a poet as well as an artist, composing the famous "Songs of Innocence" and "Songs of Experience", among others. His most famous work is a series of 21 watercolors illustrating the Book of Job. Blake moved completely away from the representational style of painting. He created his own world – a world of vivid colors, which he used subjectively, not literally – composed of strange, dramatically-posed figures set in a dreamlike environment. He used space, not naturally, but in a deliberately contrived, stylized manner. The themes of his pictures were metaphysical and religious.

Blake's followers included Samuel Palmer (1805-81), who was the best known of a group of painters called the Shoreham Ancients – artists who lived in and around Shoreham in Kent and who (for at least part of their careers) drew on the same medieval, mystical imagery.

The Swiss-born Henry Fuseli (1741-1825) was another romantic individualist whose pictures also went against convention. Some of his work bears a striking resemblance to Blake's, whom he described as "damned good to steal from". He was also strongly influenced by Michelangelo.

SATAN AROUSING THE REBEL ANGELS (PARADISE LOST)
by William Blake

Blake's early works were traditional, fitting into the Neoclassical style, but his later pictures, such as the one illustrated, show the full effect of his individual romantic direction, influenced by medieval imagery, and the Mannerist forms of the later Renaissance.

Like Fuseli, Blake was inspired by literature. He admired particularly the works of Dante and Milton. Blake also came under the influence of Michelangelo and the figures in this painting demonstrate the same dramatic poses and expressions.

At the beginning of his career, Blake was an engraver, and this can be seen in his absolute sureness of line. Engravers describe space and shading by varying the thickness of the line, because they are largely dependent on linear representation. This picture demonstrates how Blake has been able, with professional ease, to exploit this facility. Many of Blake's watercolors are colored drawings, with a strong, fluid pen and ink outline. His color and his interpretation are subjective and imaginative, yet very subtle; occasionally being little more than tinted tone. Blake refused to copy nature, which he said would result in nothing but, "blots and blurs"; instead, he relied upon visions and the power of his imagination.

Strangely, Blake was little appreciated in his own lifetime; his work was controversial, and often criticized. But, despite his lack of popular appeal, Blake influenced artists within his own circle; he has also had a tremendous impact on 20th century painting and illustration, and today his followers are numerous.

EARLY SOCIETIES

DESPITE THE GROWING use of watercolor by major artists during the 18th century, the art institutions still had to be convinced that watercolor was not an inferior medium to oil. The Royal Academy in London, for example, in the early years of the 19th century, still gave the best positions to oils and miniatures. In addition, those who painted only in watercolor were not admitted to membership.

Watercolorists reacted by forming societies where they could hold their own exhibitions. The first group, formed in 1804, was known as the Old Watercolor Society. Its shows were so successful that competition among members for recognition and exhibition spaces, combined with the Society's tendency towards exclusiveness led to the establishment, in 1807, of a rival institution: the New Society of Painters in Miniature and Watercolors.

The careers of several painters form a bridge across this transition period. John Varley is typical of them. His prolific output influenced not only the Society's exhibitions, but also the work of other artists, such as John Sell Cotman, David Cox, and Peter de Wint.

English watercolors were exhibited at the Paris World's Fair in 1855 and this helped the medium to achieve wider popularity throughout Europe. Critics expressed a lively interest in the 114 English watercolors on display in Paris. They noted that artists of the first rank in England were devoting much time to producing watercolors as finished works; and that some of these pictures possessed the vigor of oil paintings, thus demonstrating the versatility of the medium. The French journalist Edmond About drew his readers' attention to the fact that there were two societies in London devoted to encouraging and selling watercolors. Although the use of watercolor was by no means new to continental European artists, watercolor paintings came to be regarded for a while as an "English" contribution to the contemporary art scene.

Gradually, the English art establishment began to accept watercolor as an art form in its own right; yet this was still a long process. Attitudes could not be changed quickly: for instance, the Old Society eventually received permission from Queen Victoria to add the word "Royal" to its name, but this was not until 1881, after the deaths of some of its major contributors.

RHYL SANDS
by David Cox

David Cox (1783-1859) had been an enthusiastic pupil of Varley's. But this blustery, atmospheric scene contains a new freedom. Cox was one of a group of new members who joined the Old Society early in the second decade of the 19th century. Their adventurous use of color breathed fresh life into British watercolor, but it also exposed them to criticism. Cox, for instance, was accused of being hasty and careless. He liked to work on a rough, slightly off-white paper, which absorbed color wash, and has since become known as "Cox paper". He applied a preliminary wash over pencil, or charcoal, and then built up more washes, using a very wet, rich color. The brushstrokes in the foreground are shorter, designed to add careful detail. Specks of the rough paper beneath tend to show through the pictures. The overall effect is one of spontaneity.

WALTHAM ABBEY
by John Varley

This is a craftsmanlike picture done by a man who, though sometimes criticized, was undoubtedly a powerful figure in the development of watercolor painting. John Varley (1778–1842) was acknowledged as a great teacher, who published a series of books on the techniques of painting, such as Principles of Landscape Painting, *and a* Practical Treatise on the Art of Drawing in Perspective. *His work inspired thousands of amateurs to wander the countryside with sketchbooks, and to try their hand at watercolors which, owing to their portability and to the speed with which they could be applied, were ideally suited to hobbyists, as well as professional artists.*

Varley became an artist, as did his younger brother Cornelius, despite stubborn opposition from a middle-class father. One of the original members of the Old Watercolor Society, Varley perfected such techniques as the laying down of interrelated color washes, to form an overall harmony of effect. His careful juxtaposition of light and shade can be seen in this picture.

One of Varley's most quoted remarks, "Nature wants cooking", stressed the importance he attached to the refinement of nature, and to the attention which artists should pay to detail when painting a picture. He also recommended that every picture should contain a "look-there" – a focal point to attract the eye. In this picture, for example, the viewer is invited to look straight down the road, past the figure entering the shadow of the tree.

Varley was one of the most prolific watercolor painters, and his work tends to become repetitive – the same subjects and themes appear again and again. In addition, some pictures seem less inspired and energetic than others. Nevertheless, Varley was undoubtedly a major contributor to the art of watercolor painting, influencing the work of many other artists.

RECOGNITION

THERE WAS GENERALLY more encouragement for watercolor painters to explore their own avenues as the 19th century advanced, than there had been when the medium was becoming established. With watercolor now widely used and recognized, painters began to think of themselves as mainstream artists, rather than as members of a new minority medium. One of the consequences of this attitude was that artists began to develop a markedly individual approach, even if they were associated with a group. For instance, Samuel Palmer, although linked with the Shoreham Ancients (*see pp 38-9*), is recognized as an artist with a distinct personal style.

This new confidence meant that many artists began to break away from the rigid confines of accepted working methods – by combining various mediums, and by mixing watercolor with body color. Palmer, for instance, liked to use thick gouache and, on occasion, to mix oil, ink and watercolor in the same painting. Constable,

although primarily an oil painter, used watercolors and gouache – mainly for his weather and sky pictures.

There was also a tendency for painters to concentrate on British landscape rather than looking to the continent of Europe. The main reason for this was simple. The French Revolution and the Napoleonic Wars meant that European travel became increasingly hazardous.

From a 20th century vantage point, it is possible to identify groups of "local" artists. The Norwich School, for example, centered around East Anglia and included artists such as Cotman and John Crome (1768-1821). Cotman, however, is also associated with Yorkshire, where he spent his most fertile and fruitful period. Constable found endless inspiration in the hedgerows and soft countryside of his native Suffolk. Palmer and his followers in Kent became associated with Shoreham and the surrounding countryside, while de Wint fell in love with his wife's home county of Lincolnshire.

BRIDGE OVER A TRIBUTARY OF THE WITHAM RIVER IN LINCOLNSHIRE
by Peter de Wint

The dominant feeling in the watercolors of Peter de Wint (1784-1849) is one of tranquility. The Lincolnshire landscape was his favorite subject; his wife's family came from the county town of Lincoln, and the artist's best work was painted in the vicinity.

De Wint trained as an apprentice with the mezzotint-engraver, J.R. Smith. Later he met Varley and through Dr. Monro, he was influenced by Girtin. De Wint was one of the second generation of artists who joined the Old Watercolor Society and then played a major role in establishing high standards for English watercolor. De Wint's style, once established, remained constant for most of his life.

This painting of the bridge and the woman has been done with great affection, which gives the scene a feeling of intimacy. It illustrates de Wint's brilliant technique in depicting the surface of the water, and is also a fine example of his robust mastery of color. The artist has produced a scene which is aglow with warm tones; contrast is provided by a cool, pale sky. The viewer's attention is concentrated on a luminous semi-circular zone under the arch of the bridge, which is reflected in the water.

De Wint applied rich colors in washes with a loaded brush. He then used a sharp instrument, possibly the end of the brush, to scratch highlights into the color, causing the white paper to show through. These touches of sparkling white make the ripples on the river and the foliage in the foreground stand out, and help to bring the picture to life.

GRETA BRIDGE, YORKSHIRE
(1807) by John Sell Cotman

Cotman (1782-1842) was one of Dr. Monro's pupils (see pp 34-5). Between the ages of 21 and 23 he made three visits to Yorkshire, where he did much of his best work.

Greta Bridge *shows an understanding of form and abstract composition which makes detail unnecessary. Cotman uses washes of clear color – a technique probably learned from Varley at Dr. Monro's. The picture reveals the artist as an instinctive colorist, laying down areas of flat wash which suggest their own detail. The rocks, for example, are formed from simple washes of warm and cool colors, as are the trees. The effect is staggering – so real that the viewer tends not to notice the simple, abstract composition, the arrangement of positive and negative shapes, and the contrasts between light and dark tones.*

IN A SHOREHAM GARDEN
by Samuel Palmer

A garden is taken into a dreamlike dimension, full of glowing color, in this watercolor and gouache picture by Samuel Palmer (1805-81) – one of an extraordinary series of paintings using an approach that was later largely abandoned by the artist. The touches of gold and the white circular strokes of gouache are characteristic of work he produced between 1826 and 1835, known as his "Shoreham period".

Even without the Shoreham period, Palmer would have been a prominent painter, for he produced many conventional landscapes of high standard; some with flashes of brilliance. The son of a bookseller, he is not known to have received any formal training, yet he was exhibiting at the Royal Academy by the age of 14.

In 1824 he met Blake, who was then in his late 60s. Palmer regarded Blake as a prophet. He became one of a small group of Blake followers known as the Shoreham Ancients, and he endowed the Kent village with something of the same religiously-charged mysticism that the 20th century painter Stanley Spencer gave to the village of Cookham by the River Thames.

The Shoreham band of artists included John Linnell (later to become Palmer's father-in-law), George Richmond, Francis Oliver Finch and Edward Calvert. They saw themselves as helping to create a Golden Age; an age of romance and poetry, unhampered by materialistic considerations.

Palmer's personal visionary approach was ahead of his time, and he has had a great impact on the 20th century. The technique used here is essentially modern, but the feeling evoked by the figure and the composition seems to take the viewer back to medieval times – an atmosphere which pervades many of his Shoreham paintings.

WILLIAM MORRIS

(The Pre-Raphaelite Movement)

THE "PRE-RAPHAELITE BROTHERHOOD", a movement which looked back romantically to what they believed was an inspired golden age before Raphael, emerged in the late 19th century in open revolt against the current art establishment. Rich colors, ornamentation, and extravagant detail were introduced into their work, and some leading Pre-Raphaelites were grand experimenters in watercolor. The artists of this movement made their entrance with a flourish upon a rather conservative scene, and were initially often laughed at, although they later became extremely popular.

Leading figures among the Pre-Raphaelites were William Holman Hunt, Dante Gabriel Rossetti, Edward Burne-Jones and John Everett Millais. Many of their pictures have a distinctly medieval flavor – the viewer almost expects to see distant castle towers among the hills and trees of their miniature landscape backgrounds – combined with a sense of magical legend. One of their aims was to fuse poetry and romance with full, colorful illustration. In order to achieve this, they allowed their imaginations to roam freely, but at the same time they adhered strictly to traditional skills. Their drawing, for instance, was of the highest standard, while they became experts at using and adapting a wide range of materials.

The Pre-Raphaelite movement worked mainly in oils, but when they used watercolor it was not usually in the traditional manner of transparent washes and working from light to dark. Instead artists often used color densely, with as little water as possible, building up detail until the paint was uncoventionally thick. They also worked in gouache, exploiting its opaque properties to create the same dense, detailed image. It is, in fact, quite difficult to differentiate between their gouaches and watercolors and their oils.

Looking back, it is possible to see a fluctuating development, from Blake through Samuel Palmer to the Pre-Raphaelites, of a magical theme, an attempt to transport viewers from the mundane, material world into a spiritual and idealistic universe, populated by figures from religious, mythical and romantic legends. Embodied in the Pre-Raphaelite pictures, however, decorating the tableaux of imagined and legendary events and forming the background, is a loyalty to nature which called for painstaking reproduction in precise detail of foliage, fruit, flowers and animals.

William Morris (1834-96) became closely linked with the Pre-Raphaelites, and under his influence they took a new direction; still in rebellion, but this time against the drab uniformity of industrial production.

Morris studied architecture, then painting, and later became committed to design. He believed that mass-production methods denied people the opportunity of developing their full potential. In an attempt to change this, he formed a company, Morris and Co., to produce beautifully designed decorations that would transform the interiors of 19th century homes. He produced carpets, tapestries, wallpaper, other textiles and glass, with the help of artists such as Burne-Jones. Morris also founded the Kelmscott Press in 1890 with the aim of producing well-designed books. Although Morris introduced a new and influential movement in design, he remained traditional in his use of heavy colors and full decoration.

AVON CHINTZ
by William Morris

The intertwined flowers and foliage, reminiscent of the illuminated manuscripts of early Celtic and Christian art, form part of Morris's attempt to change the face of a society that he felt had become gray and inhuman. He frequently employed watercolor for his working designs.

BOTANICAL ART

WATERCOLOR HAS BEEN widely employed in the service of science. This is because the medium allows colors and tones to be built up gradually to precise requirements, making it exactly right for the execution of the tiny details of plants and animals.

The first botanical painters compiled herbals, books of remedies based on herbs, which were popular in most European countries. The purpose of their paintings was not to decorate the herbals, but to make it easier to identify the plants. A notable example is the Italian *Dioscorides* herbal (c. 512) which contains many plates painted with an opaque color akin to gouache, while the Carrara herbal (c. 1400) is even better known.

When the Western world's interest in science was reawakened at the time of the Renaissance, a host of botanical painters began recording the minute characteristics of thousands of species. However, these painters did not regard themselves as artists, but as illustrators and illuminators. Although Dürer is regarded as the first real watercolor artist, in fact these early botanical painters had used watercolor and body color long before he was born.

From the 16th century, Europe was engaged in discovering and exploring the rest of the world. Botanists and scientists – such as Jacques Le Moyne de Morgues, who went to Florida in 1564, and his colleague John White – travelled far and wide, producing paintings of exotic flora and fauna, which were often the only means of bringing their discoveries home. Another of these adventurers was Mrs. Sibylla Merian (1647-1717) whose paintings of Surinam provide a unique record of its flowers, vegetables, insects and birds.

The Dutch trade in Asia opened up new possibilities for this type of watercolor painting. The flowers and plants of Ceylon, Bengal, Java and Japan, for example, were drawn and painted by a German, Engelbert Kaempfer, who travelled as a surgeon with the Dutch East India Company. Similarly, trade paved the way for botanical painters to record the flora and fauna of Africa and the West Indies.

The 18th century – the Age of Enlightenment – with its revived interest in plants, horticulture, art and travel, was also the age of sponsors and benefactors. Sir Joseph Banks, president of the Royal Society from 1743 to 1820, was especially interested in botany. Under his auspices, artists were encouraged to go abroad – Alexander Buchan and Sydney Parkinson, for instance, accompanied James Cook on the *Endeavor* – and under his patronage the Bauer brothers, Francis and Ferdinand, were able to leave Germany and work in England.

Today, colored botanical illustrations are almost always done in watercolor, or gouache. The teaching methods of art colleges specializing in scientific illustration have changed little since the early masters; the emphasis is still on strict observation and the ability to produce a technically correct, yet visually pleasing, image.

HOG PLUM (*SPONDIAS MOMBIN*)
(c. 1700) by Maria Sibylla Merian

Mrs. Merian used watercolor and body color on vellum. She was essentially a student of insects, but even when the plant is a secondary subject, her paintings are worthy of recognition as botanical records. Although Mrs. Merian was a talented draftswoman, with untiring powers of observing detail, she painted with imaginative flair. As a result she almost creates another, vivid, world in which the characteristics of the plants are strictly accurate, yet somehow larger than life, with insects forming an integral part of these imaginative tableaux.

The daughter of a Swiss engraver, Matthaus Merian, Mrs. Merian too engraved some of her paintings. While staying at a convent in Holland, Mrs. Merian saw a collection of South American insects, and decided that one day she would go and paint the living ones. In 1698, aged 51, she set off with her daughter for Surinam, where she was to spend two years drawing and painting the wild life. Her collection of paintings was published under the title Metamorphosis Insectorum Surinamensium.

ELLEBORE OILLET
from: **Les Choix de plus Belles Fleures**
(1827-33) by Pierre-Joseph Redouté

The Frenchman, Pierre-Joseph Redouté (1759-1840) produced some of the world's most beautiful plant portraits. Redouté's supreme opportunity came when the Empress Josephine employed him to record the vast range of flowers in the gardens of her chateau of Malmaison. From this commission and later work came the series of books which were to establish Redouté's reputation. The latest contemporary techniques in color printing were used in producing the books; some of these techniques, involving advanced methods of stipple engraving, were developed by Redouté himself.

Ellebore.

Oillet.

P. J. Redouté.

Langlois.

CABBAGE ROSE (*ROSA CENTIFOLIA*)
by Jan van Huysum

This watercolor, done in layers of transparent wash, is very different from the colored drawings of many horticultural illustrators. Jan van Huysum (1682-1749) was essentially a flower painter rather than an illustrator. His work includes drawings, watercolors and oils.

Van Huysum's watercolors are loosely painted. The brushstrokes alone describe the forms of the petals and leaves, while the background is washed in behind the flowers, immediately giving the picture
a sense of space. Imperfections and irregularities on the leaves are faithfully portrayed, in contrast to some of the early Dutch oil paintings of flowers, where each flower head was arranged so that it faced the painter and did not obscure any of the others.

Horticulture became well established in Europe during the 17th century; wild flowers were propagated for use in gardens while new plants were introduced from other countries. This growing interest stimulated a demand for portraits of the new flowers, and Holland became an important center of this genre.

SPONTANEITY

THE DIFFERENCE BETWEEN a watercolor sketch and a watercolor painting is often a fine one. In general, it is impossible to decide by looking at a work, since a painting which appears to be merely a sketchy image could well be a finished picture. The definition really lies in the intention behind the work; usually a sketch is done for reference, as a quick recording of a scene or event which the artist intends to use in a more finished product later.

Before watercolor gained status as a medium in its own right, it was often used as a means of making preliminary sketches for an anticipated oil painting. In fact, watercolor has never quite relinquished this role; it is still a convenient, compact way of making color sketches. Frequently such sketches become as well known as the finished painting; while, on other occasions, the finished picture is lost or destroyed, and only the sketches survive.

During the era of the Grand Tour, which reached its peak in the 18th century (*see pp 30-1*), the tourist's equivalent of the modern camera was needed. A watercolor sketch could be done quickly, either by the young aristocrat on tour – refining his artistic talents – or by a painter, engaged for that purpose.

A host of famous painters have used watercolors to make preliminary sketches – among the best known collections are those done by Eugène Delacroix on his African journey in 1832. The pages of his sketchbooks reveal a magical insight into Arab life: tiny thumbnail sketches record details of market places, Moorish interiors and domestic items. Delacroix used these sketchbooks as the basis for later oil paintings; none of them however retained the charm of these early miniature color sketches.

Gouache is particularly useful in the sketching role, it has a directness and immediacy, which allows the artist to lay down very strong opaque colors quickly and accurately. One artist who made extensive use of gouache was Gwen John, whose simple color sketches are becoming increasingly respected.

**VIEW OVER A WIDE LANDSCAPE
WITH TREES IN THE FOREGROUND**
by John Constable

Constable (1776-1837), more than any other 19th century painter, understood the English skies with their ever-changing weather patterns. He once declared: "The sky is the keynote, the standard of scale, and the chief organ of sentiment – it governs everything." Constable's interest in cloud formations and in weather patterns went further than his paintings. He studied the subject, becoming familiar with the

meanings of certain formations and indications. It is known, for instance, that he was influenced by Luke Howard's The Climate of London.

Constable's reputation as an oil painter has overshadowed his skills in watercolor, although it was in watercolor that he was best able to record the transient effects of wind, rain and sun. His watercolors were seldom exhibited until recently, however.

This watercolor sketch is one of hundreds of studies made by the artist, to capture the atmospheric seasonal and temperate effects of the English weather.

A STOUT LADY, AND OTHERS, IN CHURCH
(1913-25) by Gwen John

This quick pencil and wash picture, based on a drawing sketched hurriedly in church, has been done with the economy of detail, line and color that watercolor allows; yet it contains a wealth of information. Rarely can so much atmosphere have been captured so quickly with a pencil and brush.

Gwen John (1876-1939) wrote, "People are like shadows to me and I am like a shadow". In this picture not only the people, but the shapes between them are washed in with a shadowy quality. Gwen John made hundreds of watercolor and gouache sketches similar to this one. She had become religious, and was fascinated by the congregation at the church in Meudon outside Paris where she worshipped at this period in her life.

Most of the gouaches of this series cannot be precisely dated, but they all reveal the influence of Japanese prints. However, the abstracted compositions, patterns and simplified shapes are never allowed to detract from the subject; instead they enhance it.

GIRL CARRYING A PALM FROND
(1927-32) by Gwen John

This charcoal and gouache sketch of a young girl clutching a palm frond – probably at a Palm Sunday ceremony – has been executed in subdued colors. Once again, it reveals the influence on Gwen John of Japanese art. She has used simple, flat, graceful shapes, with very little actual form indicated in paint. This technique is reminiscent of Eastern prints, where simple, cut-out figures are placed in such a way that the shape of the background becomes an important part of the composition.

With a minimum number of brushstrokes, the artist has captured the churchlike atmosphere, the silent solemnity of the occasion and the solitude of the young girl. Gwen John has built up the background in short, vertical strokes of color, in exactly the same way that she does in her oil paintings. She has achieved this by taking advantage of the opacity of the gouache paint, using very little water, and applying the color in broken areas, thus allowing the colored ground to show through.

Gwen John lived an obscure life, and her talent was largely unrecognized until very recent times. For instance, a series of her later gouaches, watercolors and sketches – of which this is one – were thrown into a cupboard by an acquaintance, where they remained for years.

PICTURE AND WORD
ILLUSTRATION

THE ILLUSTRATION OF text by means of pictures is one of the oldest forms of art, and watercolor has been associated with it from the very beginning. However, these pictures, whether on scrolls, walls or in books, were necessarily confined to a very limited number of viewers.

Even after the invention of the printing press, it was still not possible to mass-produce color illustrations. Sometimes, finished engravings were hand-tinted with watercolors, but these were understandably always restricted in number. Books containing watercolor paintings, such as botanical illustrations, were printed, but they were relatively expensive, and therefore reached only a small audience; for the cheaper mass market, printers used black and white line drawings. The history of mass illustration in the 18th and 19th centuries therefore developed independently of watercolor which, until modern times, remained a medium for paintings directed only at a comparative few. Nowadays, however, this situation has changed dramatically: technological advances mean that, for the first time, color pictures can be mass-produced.

Watercolor reproduces well; modern printing techniques can capture exactly the pale translucent character of the paint, making it difficult at times to distinguish a good quality print from the original. In addition, because oil paint takes a long time to dry, the modern illustrator almost automatically turns to watercolor or gouache, with acrylics being used occasionally.

Gouache, the "body color" favored by painters who illustrated individual books before the age of printing, has remained a major medium for illustrators because of its strength of color and opacity. Indeed, far from replacing the two traditional mediums – gouache and watercolor – modern technology has made them accessible to a vastly extended audience. The scribe who took such pains to paint the vivid watercolors accompanying his sacred texts would surely be astonished to discover that his works could now be reproduced by the million.

LES (DEUX) CONFRERES
by Honoré Daumier

An outspoken cartoonist who was imprisoned at one time for ridiculing the French king Louis Philippe, Honoré Daumier (1808-79) took an unsentimental and highly critical look at contemporary life in his illustrations for satirical journals. His illustrations had a wide influence; for instance, the work of H.K. Browne (Phiz), who illustrated for Charles Dickens, is regarded as having become sharper and better drawn after he studied Daumier's technique.

Lawyers were one of Daumier's favorite subjects, depicted with his usual ruthless and acutely-observed characterization. In this pen and ink and watercolor picture of two lawyers conferring, Daumier's skill at capturing gesture, posture and expression is self-evident. The two men lean back in happy self-satisfaction, feet stolidly implanted, in a composition which features stark contrasts between light and dark. The figures are drawn in a fluid, painterly way, with the forms being described by the brush as it applied the paint; the curving shadows and highlights emphasize the swing of the long cloaks. The cartoonist's skill in fluid drawing has brought a touch of caricature into the two bony faces, which are highlighted so that they shine with a rather sinister gleam.

THE FLOWER WINDOW
(c. 1894-7) by Carl Larsson

*This watercolor is one of the highlights of
a career devoted largely and fruitfully to
domestic culture. It belongs to a series of
illustrations entitled* Ett Hem *(The
Home) – a title which reveals much about
the artist's aims and ideals.*

*In this 19th century domestic scene, one
of the Larssons' daughters tends the plants
in the well-lit home which was the
inspiration of so many of the works by the
Swedish illustrator Carl Larsson (1853-
1919). The house, Little Hyttnäs, was the
home of Larsson and his wife Karin for
most of their married life, and it meant far
more to them than just a place in which to
live. The home itself naturally looms large
in all family life, but to the Larssons it was
also the vehicle for their creativity in design
and decoration. Together they turned the
place into a work of art, painting murals on
the walls, and decorating and collecting
with an extraordinarily individual flair.*

*"A home is not a lifeless object but a
living entity...it must keep changing from
moment to moment," wrote Larsson. "If I
should die, which oddly enough is perfectly
possible, I think to myself that our home
will go on all the same." The house has
indeed gone on, not as a home, but certainly
as a place to enjoy; it has been made into a
national museum.*

*Larsson's style of illustration was later
favored by the famous 20th century German
design center, the Bauhaus, whose members
liked the way he incorporated everyday
objects into his art, so that art merged with
life and function rather than being isolated
from it.*

*Most of Larsson's illustrations combine
washes of color with pen and ink outline.
A superb draftsman, Larsson uses line in
a way which does not flatten the image.
Secondary lines, details, and objects in the
distance are almost imperceptibly defined
with a fine drawn outline; bolder use of pen
and ink describes foreground objects and
main forms. Larsson is also selective,
choosing when not to use an outline, as can
be seen in the pattern of the runner rug on
the floor, and the striped fabric on the
wooden chair.*

BLIND GIRL WEARING FOX FUR
(1981) by Catherine Brighton

The girl's unseeing eyes stare blankly from this watercolor by Catherine Brighton (born 1943) – part of a set of illustrations for a children's book. Because the girl in the picture is blind, touch is of paramount importance, so the artist has attempted to convey the texture of all the elements in this girl's world.

The painter worked from an actual fox fur, kept in her studio for several days, to make sure she thoroughly captured its "furriness". She avoided the temptation of trying to depict every single hair, and instead painted directional brushstrokes to give an overall impression. Some areas of the watercolor paper were left to show through, in order to create highlights and to accentuate the gleam in the fox's glass eyes.

The artist always begins a picture with a line drawing in pencil on paper, which is then traced onto watercolor paper over a light-box. In pictures featuring figures, she starts with the face – the focal point which attracts the viewer's attention. She believes that the face conveys the emotion and that there is no point continuing with the rest of the painting until this is exactly right; washes of local color can then be worked into small areas, such as the brown shadows on the coat draped around the little girl.

For this picture, the artist started painting the girl's hair by building up a gray tone, leaving streaks of the white paper showing through; the main dark area of the hair was then filled in with lamp black. When this had dried, Catherine painted a thin wash of Prussian blue over the whole hair area, including the white highlights, to give that bluish sheen often seen on black hair. Unlike many watercolorists, she did not blend the washes, but waited for each area to dry before applying a new tone. The result is a precise image with crisp edges, in

contrast to another common watercolor style which aims at a blurred effect – colors are allowed to "flood" or "bleed" into each other by applying them wet on wet.

Catherine Brighton makes a living writing and illustrating picture books for young children. She says, "For me, a book begins not with a literary idea, but with an image. I see a picture in my mind, and weave the story around that".

She dislikes using photographs, and refers to them only for checking small points of technical accuracy, such as the appearance of a particular type of wheel; never as a base from which to paint a picture. She says, "People are so used to looking at photographic images that they think they are really true, but photographs form only one way of conveying what we see. A photograph gives a frozen image. With a painting, you have more control. You can set out to deliberately convey feelings, atmosphere and mood".

WATERCOLOR PAINTING IN AMERICA
THE NEW WORLD

AMERICAN ART WAS growing rapidly in sophistication by the last decades of the 18th century; and it was not long before American artists began to influence the Old World – a trend that has continued to the present day when America leads the way in many areas of Western painting. The process began when American artists went to Europe to study and work. One of the earliest of these "eastward-bound pioneers" was the Pennsylvanian-born oil painter Benjamin West (1738-1820) who first travelled through Italy and then settled in London, where he became president of the Royal Academy.

At the same time as explorers pushed into the vast interior of the American continent, artists began to paint the new landscape in all its varied aspects. For instance, the ornithologist John Audubon (1780-1851), after an education in Paris, went on numerous expeditions into the forests; the paintings of the birds he observed were to become famous not only in America, but also in Europe. Later, in the 19th century, artists recorded "the Wild West" in watercolor and oils, producing pictures which, as well as conveying an idealistic image, often showed its way of life and its landscapes with unsentimental realism.

Ironically, as the United States became increasingly confident and powerful in the second half of the 19th century, its citizens began looking towards the Old World for cultural inspiration. Works of art were imported and there was a frank and open interest in learning from the old traditions of Europe.

At the same time, watercolor in America was experiencing a surge of vigorous growth; the American Water Color Society was founded in 1866, with Samuel Colman as its first president. One of its founder members was Winslow Homer, a painter whose fresh and realistic approach marked a new stage in American art.

Homer, like many other American artists, went to the Old World for education and to gain experience before returning to America, as did Thomas Eakins and Maurice Prendergast. Other Americans remained in Europe, either permanently or for long periods, and exerted considerable influence there. Whistler, for example, settled in London in 1859; while Mary Cassatt (1844-1926) became a prominent follower of the Impressionists. John Singer Sargent (1856-1925) kept a studio in Paris and then lived mainly in England, painting portraits of celebrities such as Ellen Terry, before becoming a landscape watercolorist.

Watercolor painting in America, therefore, was not only influenced by Europe, but its envoys and emigrants played a powerful role in European art. This flow of influence in both directions across the Atlantic has continued to this day.

NEGRO BOY DANCING
by Thomas Eakins

For this watercolor of a boy dancing, watched by the man whose foot taps the rhythm, and accompanied by a youth whose body moves to the music, Eakins reversed an age-old process. Instead of drafting a quick watercolor sketch which might later be used as the basis for an oil painting, he made a preliminary study in oils as the basis for the finished watercolor picture.

Thomas Eakins (1844-1916) had an eye for detail; he enjoyed capturing the minute facts of everyday life in his paintings. Some of his pictures are reminiscent of the 18th century cartoon; not so much gross caricature or exaggeration, but that 18th century fascination with features and expressions, and with touches of sharp realism, that can freeze a moment in time, leaving behind a vivid glimpse of the past. Despite their accuracy and detail – sometimes produced by working from mathematically precise plans – Eakins' pictures are full of life and movement.

GREY AND GREEN: A SHOP IN BRITTANY
(1893) by James Abbott McNeill Whistler

This picture of a Brittany street scene bathed in sunlight has been gently interpreted by the artist in a series of subtle warm and cool tones. Unlike many of the artists of this time, Whistler (1834-1903) was concerned less with the literal content, than with the visual harmony of the paint on the paper. Here, he uses an uncontrolled technique, largely painting wet into wet washes, yet applied in a highly controlled way. The sepias, umbers and grays work together as part of a careful balance; understated, in a low tonal key.

The wet into wet technique is usually associated with spontaneity, because it is impossible to completely control the "bleeding" of the colors into each other as they dry. Whistler employed this loose approach, but the range of colors he used is very disciplined, so that the image is never really out of control, even though the picture has an impressionistic look.

The roots of this approach come from

Whistler's experience of oil painting, for he learned under Charles Gleyre, a French painter, who insisted upon a methodical approach involving careful preparation of the palette. The mixtures of paint, even of the various tones of one color, had to be kept strictly separate and neatly ordered, so that a particular tone could be related to a precise point in the painting. This is not possible with watercolors; yet Whistler applied the same strict approach to produce pictures of subtle tonal ranges, with an impressionistic freshness added by the "bleeding" effects of the watercolor.

Whistler's paintings are very atmospheric. He was sensitive to mood and weather, and although he painted a great deal in oils and pastels, his watercolors allowed him to portray subtle nuances of light and atmosphere. He was also very receptive to new ideas and was always studying other artists: Rembrandt, Corbet, the Impressionists and Japanese prints all had an enormous influence on his ideas and his work. He, in turn, affected many other painters, including Gwen John, Wilson Steer and Walter Sickert.

LOW TIDE, BEACHMONT
by Maurice Prendergast

Maurice Prendergast (1859-1924) had the American artist's liking for the factual detail of everyday life, and he was able to combine this effectively with some of the ways of interpreting and seeing which he learned in Paris. He was fascinated by typically American scenes, particularly busy streets and crowded beaches.

This picture also reveals his liking for decoration: it is a whimsical arrangement of prettily dressed girls standing among rounded rocks. The figures and the stones are treated almost as flat shapes. Prendergast's concern is with a colorful
arrangement, and the overall effect of the figures seen against the background; the composition becomes almost a piece of decorative illustration.

Prendergast studied at the Académie Julian, arriving in Paris at the age of 21, when Impressionism was in full swing. He became deeply influenced by Impressionist painting, and also by Cézanne. His choice of color and his calligraphic brushstrokes are often reminiscent of Post-Impressionist painting, of which Cézanne is a representative. In 1914, Prendergast returned to New York where he exhibited with a radical group, Los Pocho, which, in many ways, marked the beginning of a fresh era in American painting.

END OF WINTER
(1946) by Andrew Wyeth

A spiky, dead tree stands out starkly against a bleak winter landscape in a picture, which is typical of Wyeth's works at this time. Wyeth (born 1917) moved first from the comparatively broad washes of his earlier work towards a very linear style of painting, based on detailed drawings. Towards the late 1940s his choice of subjects began to settle into the rather stern landscapes for which he is best known.

Andrew Wyeth never went to art school, but was trained entirely by his father, N.C. Wyeth, an illustrator of children's classics and tales of the old Wild West, and a painter of Western and rural scenes. In 1945 Andrew's father was killed in a motor accident on a rail crossing. Wyeth has acknowledged the effect this trauma had upon him, and perhaps under this influence, his later paintings can be seen as articulating a disenchanted inner vision of the world. Many of Wyeth's paintings

show a lonely rural world, devoid of modern technology and in need of repair. His palette of greens, browns, ochres and monochromes conveys a feeling of pessimism. There is a nostalgia, perhaps, for a vanishing rural America, but there is little sentimentality in the pictures of its delapidated buildings and bare scenery.

One of Wyeth's greatest skills is his ability with drybrush technique. When using this technique the artist squeezes the excess water from the brush, dips the almost dry brush into paint diluted with a very small amount of water, and then rubs the color onto the surface; thus obtaining a much tighter control over the painting. Although the traditional watercolorist works from light to dark, allowing the surface of the paper to show through as highlights, the procedure can be varied. Some of Wyeth's watercolors employed variations on the light to dark approach, allowing him to exploit one of the most useful assets of drybrush technique – the application of very precise highlights.

PALM TREE, NASSAU
by Winslow Homer

Winslow Homer (1836-1910) left Paris too soon to be much influenced by Impressionism, yet when seen with modern hindsight his work seems to be an anticipation of that movement. His watercolors have a sense of luminous light, particularly the skies and water where, like the Impressionists, he has used broken color. The grass in the foreground of this picture is imposed red and green – an optical mixing of color in the painting rather than on the palette. This is a technique used later by some of the Impressionists, and particularly by the Neo-Impressionists.

Homer, however, is difficult to place in any movement; his pictures combine ethereal light and motion with crisp, graphic shapes which point to his training as an illustrator. Born in Boston, Massachusetts, Homer worked as an illustrator for Harper's Bazaar. *He was a correspondent during the Civil War, reporting from the front, as well as recording it in his sketchbook. Later, he travelled extensively in America, seeking its most isolated corners, and, after the age of 40 he devoted his life entirely to painting, setting out to capture scenes typical of America. Sometimes he worked in oils, but it was in watercolor that he was first able to depict the wild landscapes and seascapes which mark the best of his work.*

In this picture, Homer combines bold, direct washes, used for the sky and water, with the disciplined yet expressive brushstrokes that capture the windswept branches of the palm trees.

PAINTS

EARLY WATERCOLORS were manufactured as hard sticks, and were rubbed onto the palette with water to extract the color. Today, the colors come in three main forms: pans, tubes and cakes. You can also buy liquid watercolor in bottles; opaque color – such as gouache and poster color – in jars; and watercolor pencils.

Watercolors are basically pigments which have been mixed with water and gum arabic (to bind them together), glycerine (to stop the paint from cracking), and a preservative. It is sometimes said that watercolors tend to fade, but this is an unfair simplification, as in fact some pigments are more stable and permanent than others. Among the very durable colors are the umbers, the siennas, viridian, ceruleum blue, cobalt blue, terre verte and yellow ochre. On the other hand, chrome yellow, carmine and Vandyke brown are notoriously fugitive, and do not age well.

Watercolor

True watercolor contains no opaque substances and is, therefore, transparent. The best is made from real pigments and is often referred to as "artist's" quality. It is more expensive than

lower grade, or "student", paint, but the colors are more vivid, which means that almost all professional and experienced painters use the superior product. "Student" quality watercolors are frequently made with cheaper, substitute pigments; such colors are often called "fugitive" and cannot be relied on not to fade.

When buying paints for the first time it is a good idea to choose at least a few basic colors from the "artist's" range. There really is a difference, and it would be a pity to judge the medium without experiencing some of the better quality pigments. "Student" paints are useful if you feel you want to try a new color, yet are not quite sure whether you will like it. Experiment with the cheaper paints; if you get on well with certain colors, buy the "artist's" version next time round.

Compressed powder cakes are the cheapest form of watercolor paint. They are slow to use, in the sense that it takes a long time to moisten the paint sufficiently with the brush to produce a dense color.

Look after your paints: watercolors last for a long time if you treat them well. Always replace the lids of tube color. If you do not, the paint will go hard very quickly. Should you accidently allow this to happen, do not abandon the paint; in an emergency, you can cut open the tube and use it as an improvised pan. Pans, too, can become very dry and hard; when this happens, a few drops of water will revive the paint.

Gouache and poster color

Also known as "body color", gouache is an opaque type of watercolor made from more coarsely ground pigment than that used in the manufacture of pure watercolor. The lighter colors are made by adding white pigment, and the paint dries to an opaque, matt finish. Gouache is a lively, direct medium, and is as well suited to tightly rendered work as it is to looser color sketching. Its main advantage is that it can be worked "light over dark" (*see pp 204-5*). The opacity also makes gouache suitable for working on toned and colored papers. Poster colors possess the same dense, matt qualities as gouache, but are cruder and come in a comparatively limited range of colors.

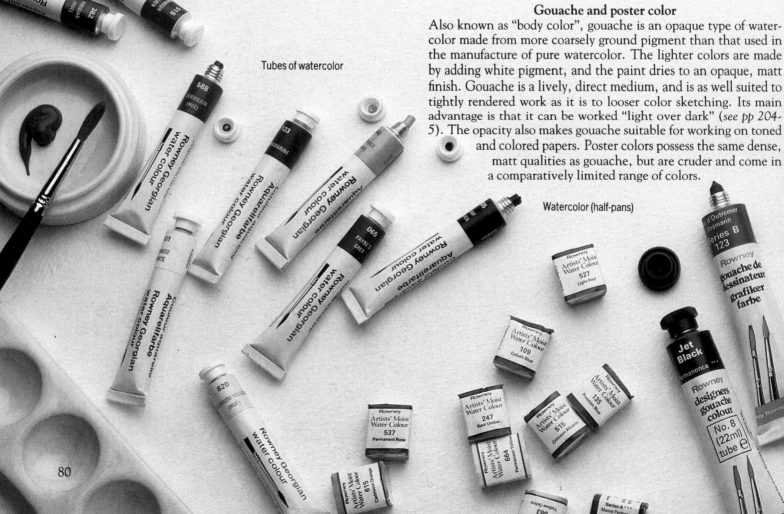

Tubes of watercolor

Watercolor (half-pans)

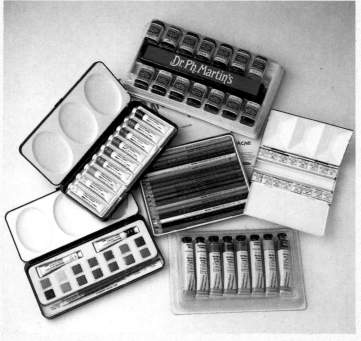

Watercolor, gouache, watercolor pencils, and concentrates are all available in sets. These provide a convenient basic palette, which can be expanded gradually as you gain more experience.

All watercolor paints are laboratory-tested to ensure that their color, consistency, and transparency remain constant. Most manufacturers indicate each color's degree of permanency as follows: permanent; normally permanent; moderately permanent; or fugitive

Liquid watercolor

Some watercolors are manufactured in liquid form: they are often highly concentrated and come in bottles, usually with their own "eye-dropper" for adding controlled amounts of color to water. Concentrated color can be fugitive – some pigments fade quickly. It is, however, popular with designers and illustrators because of its exceptionally bright and glowing colors. Moreover, if the work is intended for reproduction only, the life-span of the original is usually less important.

Sets and boxes

As well as being sold as individual tubes, pans, cakes and jars, all the different watercolor types can be bought in sets and boxes. Paintboxes are invaluable for outdoor work, enabling you to slip your entire watercolor equipment into an inside pocket and carry it around with you. Sets of paints – tubes packaged in wooden or cardboard boxes – are also very convenient and make ideal presents.

Watercolor pencils

To combine line with areas of wash, choose watercolor pencils. This comparatively new medium, a cross between colored pencils and watercolor paint, is available in a wide range of colors.

Gouache

Watercolor pencils

Poster color

BRUSHES

ALL WATERCOLOR brushes are softer than the brushes used for oil painting. There are two main categories available: natural and man-made. What follows is your guide to choosing the best.

Without question, the best watercolor brush you can buy is the so-called sable brush. The hairs for this come from the tail of the kolinsky, or Siberian weasel, which explains why such brushes are expensive. If properly maintained, however, sable brushes can last for a very long time, thus making their cost worthwhile.

What makes sable brushes so distinctive? To start with, they have a springiness and pliancy all of their own – qualities that lend themselves to lively, yet controlled brushstrokes. It is this facility that cheaper brushes find difficult to imitate. Sable brushes also absorb and hold paint well, while keeping their perfectly pointed shape.

To keep prices down, some manufacturers mix sable with other hairs and bristles, such as hair from the ears of oxen. Brushes made with squirrel hair, or ox hair not mixed with sable are cheaper still; of the two the ox hair variety is generally considered to be superior. Hair from goats, camels and mongoose is also sometimes used.

Synthetic watercolor brushes fall roughly into two types: soft ones with a texture and flexibility intended to mimic the qualities of natural hair; and all-purpose nylon brushes, which are suitable for watercolor, oil, or acrylic painting.

Brush shapes

All brushes consist of a head bound to a wooden handle by means of a metal ferrule. You can judge the quality of a brush by examining the condition of its bristles – these should be firmly pointed with no odd hairs straying out of place.

Brushes with a round ferrule are known as "round brushes"; if the ferrule is slightly flattened they are termed "flat" brushes. "Filberts" are brushes with bristles which have been cut off at the end to create a flat, chisel-like head; while "brights" have shorter bristles, giving them greater spring and control.

Specialist brushes

Special brushes are designed to produce particular effects; for example, the smooth "boneless" shapes which give Chinese and

a Thin, flat "Brights"

b Wash brush

c Long-handled Fan

d Rigger

e Oriental brushes

Japanese watercolors their distinctive quality are produced by specific brushes. These bamboo or cane-handled brushes can be useful for applying washes and flecks of color, but they are not always suitable for work outside the Oriental styles.

Watercolor artists often use fan-shaped brushes for blending colors. They come in various sizes. There are several larger brushes designed specifically for flat washes and, although expensive, they are indispensible when it comes to covering large flat areas of color. The dabber, with its full rounded head of bristles, is a popular example.

Bristle brushes, normally used with oils or acrylics, are stiffer than the typical watercolor brush, making them useful for scrubbing out lighter areas and for the correction of mistakes.

For linear techniques and drawing with watercolor, artists often use long, tapering brushes. These brushes, sometimes known as "riggers", are designed for lettering and poster writing. Miniatures and finer detail can be done with specialist sable brushes, known as "retouching" brushes. They have particularly short bristles. Small decorators' brushes are useful for painting large areas and for some special effects, such as splattering. Stencil brushes, made from hard-wearing bristles, are ideal for stippling as well as stencilling.

BRUSHES
a "Brights", for lively, controlled brushwork; **b** Wash brush, for flat expanses; **c** Fan, for blending; **d** Rigger, for line and calligraphic brushstrokes; **e** Oriental brushes, for flowing, undulating line; **f** Rounds, for general purpose watercolor work; **g** Synthetic brushes make inexpensive alternatives; **h** Mop brush, for textural washes, such as sky and water.

Brush sizes

Standard brush sizes normally range from 00 to 12 or 14, the 00 representing the smallest size. Some manufacturers have a larger size, while some produce an 000 for particularly fine work.

The size of some flat brushes is expressed as bristle width. One series, for instance, runs from 5mm (¼in) to 25mm (1in).

Brush care

Every time you use a brush, you should rinse it out with water; after finishing a painting session, clean your brushes thoroughly with mild soap and warm water. Shake the brushes into their natural shape – do not squeeze them – and allow them to dry naturally. It is very difficult to get a brush back into its proper shape if you do not take these steps.

Many brushes are sold with small plastic protectors that fit over the bristles. Do not make the mistake of throwing these protectors away; instead you should always use them to keep your brushes well protected, until you actually need them.

f Sable Rounds

g Synthetic brushes

h Mop brush

83

SUPPORTS

THE "SUPPORT" IS the artist's working surface – the material on which the picture is painted. Fortunately for the watercolorist, this means paper, which is economic in price, conveniently and commonly available, and easy to carry around.

The support is extremely important to a watercolor painter, as it plays an active and direct role in the making of a picture. Watercolor paper comes in a wide variety of weights, textures, colors and quality. In many cases, the texture itself is an integral part of the picture, its roughness showing through in the form of speckles, and adding a touch of spontaneity and liveliness. In this way, for example, tiny specks of highlight can be added to a sky, light shining through leaves can be made more luminous, and sunlight can be given a more realistic shimmering effect.

Colored papers are often combined with gouache, their color being incorporated into the picture. Pure watercolor is sometimes used on very pale tinted paper, but this means that you lose the effect of the bright white highlights.

Most watercolor paper has a right side and a wrong side. The correct side, on which the texture is carefully prepared, is usually coated with size (*see glossary*). If you hold up the paper and inspect it, you will notice that the grain on the correct side has a more natural, less symmetrical, appearance, while on the wrong side the grain is more regular.

The best paper is hand-made from pulped linen rag, which has been skilfully processed to eliminate impurities, and then coated with size from an animal glue solution. Hand-made papers can be recognized by the maker's watermark; also they often have irregular edges, as opposed to the smooth clean-cut edges of papers which have been machine-made from wood pulp.

If you are starting out as a watercolorist, it is probably advisable to avoid some of the more extremely textured, or coarse-grained paper. This type, which has an extra rough surface, is popular with many artists, but can sometimes present the beginner with problems, because it is much more difficult to control the paint as it washes onto the irregular support. However, when you become more experienced, this type of paper can produce a beautiful, luminous sparkle through the washes, because the paint sinks into the pitted surface and leaves speckles untouched.

Cold-pressed and hot-pressed

The most common watercolor paper, and the type usually recommended for beginners, is a semi-rough, medium-quality paper. Usually known as "cold-pressed", it is also sometimes described by the odd-sounding term "not" paper, because it has not undergone the alternative process of hot-pressing. Also popular among many very experienced artists, cold-pressed paper is intended as a compromise to suit different methods of working; its slightly textured surface gives some spontaneity to washes, but will also receive line well, and is suitable for fine, detailed brushwork.

Hot-pressed paper is designed to provide a suitable support for drawings. This fine-grained paper is pressed while hot to straighten it, and its hard smooth surface is ideal for drawings in pencil, pen and ink, or line and wash. Some watercolor artists like its uncompromisingly slippery surface, which can make washes slide

Whatman Rough

Whatman Not

Whatman H.P.

Waterford Rough

Waterford Not

Waterford H.P.

Bockingford

and spread rapidly, as well as increasing the luminosity of colors. Many artists, however, find that it is not absorbent enough for conventional watercolor painting.

Stretching the support

Unless watercolor paper is either thick, or ready-mounted (*see below*), it can be warped by the application of paints and water. You may, therefore, wish to stretch any thinner, or unmounted paper before use.

First, place the sheet of paper in a tray of water, or hold it under the faucet, until it is thoroughly wet. Then carefully shake off excess water and place the paper on your drawing board. The board should be larger in area than the paper, and thick enough not to warp as wet paper dries upon it. When placing the paper on the board, make sure that the correct side faces upwards. Now stretch the paper slightly, holding it with both hands. Immediately after wetting and stretching, stick the edges of the paper to the board with strips of gum-backed tape. For extra strength, pin the corners of the paper and tape to the board with thumbtacks, then leave the paper to dry naturally.

The main reason for stretching paper is to prevent it from wrinkling when it is wetted. However, papers vary in weight and the heaviest ones can sometimes be used without stretching them first. Paper has traditionally been measured in pounds per ream (480 or 500 sheets) and this is still in common use. However, the official metric measure is grams per square meter (gsm or gm). As a guide, thin paper may be referred to as weighing 70 pounds (150gsm), while a heavier grade would be perhaps 140 pounds (285gsm). Some of the toughest papers can be stretched on special frames, rather like those for stretching canvas, but these are unsuitable for thinner papers.

Some artists stretch their paper on thinner boards, or card, for easy transportation. However, the card can warp as the wet, stretched paper dries, although this can be offset by stretching the paper on both sides of the card.

Ready-prepared watercolor boards – thin paper mounted by being glued onto sturdy pieces of card – are available if you want to avoid stretching your own paper. These will keep their shape while you are painting, and they are available in pads, usually of about 25 sheets each.

SURFACES
Watercolor papers are specially made to meet the exacting requirements of particular techniques and to produce specific effects. The artist's choice depends largely on the subject, the techniques used, and the effect required. There are three basic types of paper in general use: Rough, Not, and Hot Pressed (H.P.)
Photograph Tif Hunter

Georgian

Cartridge

Greens RWS Rough

Greens RWS Not

Greens RWS H.P.

Greens Camber Sand Not

Greens Turner Grey Not

Greens De Wint Rugged

EASELS

THE WATERCOLOR ARTIST needs an easel which is easy to carry, easy to pack, and which has a strong enough grip to hold a board on which the watercolor paper is fixed. One of the most popular choices for general use – the studio easel – has a heavy wooden frame, clamps, and wheels. It can be used for watercolors if necessary, but easels designed like this tend to have frames fixed in a vertical position, which is not really best suited to watercolor. The watercolor artist usually finds it easier to have a work surface which can be tilted, so that wet washes can be applied when the board is horizontal, and details painted in when the board is adjusted to a convenient angle.

Tabletop easels

A vast variety of easels is now available for artists, many of which are suitable for watercolorists. One of the most popular is almost a miniature version of the studio easel, except that it is specifically designed for use on a tabletop, and therefore has no wheels. It also has sloping back-struts which enable the main frame to be tilted to the desired angle. However, this type of easel will not generally allow the support to be lowered completely to the horizontal.

Another tabletop easel is much simpler: it consists basically of a frame to hold the board, which is propped up on deckchair-type slats at the rear, giving a wide but limited range of tilted angles. Like the previous one, this type usually comes in wood. It often has pads on the bottom, to prevent it from slipping. It is ideal for the home or studio, because it can be so easily moved about, and the board can be rested on it without being clamped, making it simple to remove and place on a flat surface.

Standing easels

The watercolor artist can also make use of an easel designed in the simple, "blackboard holder" style, with two legs in front, and an adjustable one at the back, and often with broad "shelves" or "height trays" on which to rest the watercolor board. However, all the types mentioned are essentially indoor easels; if you take them outdoors you will need to find an almost perfectly flat piece of ground on which to place them.

Outdoor easels

Some of the best of these are made of light metal, with individually adjustable legs. They can be set up to a standing height, they have a moveable bar with clamps for fixing the board and tilting it at any angle from flat to vertical, and they can be folded to almost umbrella-like proportions for carrying. Wooden easels with adjustable legs are heavier to carry, but may have stable wooden trays on which paints and water can be rested.

Probably the most popular of all is the wooden box easel. This combines a traditional collapsible easel with a wooden box for carrying painting equipment. The box transforms into a deep combined tray/tabletop which can be used for paints, palettes, water, and other materials.

EASELS
a Salisbury "box easel" – folding and versatile for many types of work; **b** Canterbury – lightweight, folding easel; **c** St Pauls – similar to Canterbury, but with supports for a box; **d** Westminster – metal, folding easel.

TABLE EASEL
A compact easel, ideal where space is limited. This model is adjustable and can be set at any angle

Photograph Tif Hunter

OTHER EQUIPMENT

APART FROM THE materials and equipment already mentioned in previous sections, you will also need a number of miscellaneous items, most of which are illustrated on this page.

Graphite drawing pencils range from very hard to very soft: the softer the pencil, the darker and more feathery the strokes; while a hard pencil produces a pale, thin line. You will probably use a B or 2B most of the time.

A good quality drawing board will last a lifetime and is a worthwhile investment. However, you can make your own, provided that the wood is sturdy and will not warp or bend.

Mediums and additives

The only additive you actually need for painting in watercolor is some clean water, but there are various substances which can be mixed with the paint, or water to produce specific effects, or make the application of color easier.

One of the most popular is *gum arabic*, which can be added to the paint as you work. Too much will make the paint slippery and jelly-like; but in moderation it enlivens the texture of the paint and enhances the vividness of the colors.

Gum water, is a thinner alternative which improves the flow of the paint and also brightens the colors. A little *glycerine* prolongs the drying time of paint, which is particularly useful when working one color into another while the paint is still wet; it also counteracts the drying effect of sunlight and central heating. If you want to speed up the drying time of paint, add a 96% solution of *alcohol* to the water. A small amount of refined *oxgall* poured into the water will improve the flow and adhesiveness of paint. To create specific areas of white, apply *masking fluid* with a brush and allow it to dry. Color can now be safely applied. When this is dry, rub off the masking fluid with your finger, or an eraser to reveal the crisp white shapes beneath. Special purpose *varnish* will protect the picture surface without adversely affecting the painting, and help to bring out the resonance and brilliance of the colors. However, purists argue that varnish changes the traditionally dull, matt watercolor finish.

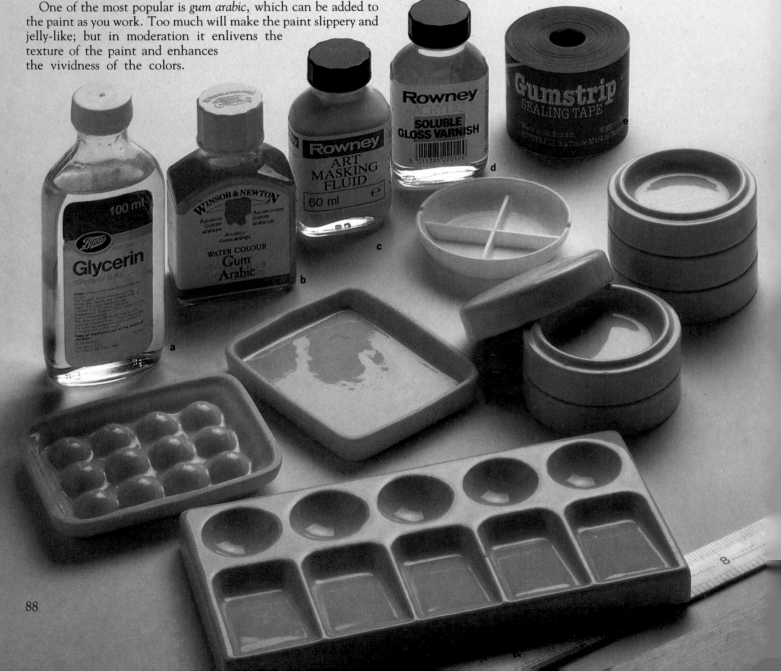

a gum arabic; **b** glycerine; **c** masking fluid; **d** special purpose varnish; **e** gum-backed tape; **f** palettes come in a variety of shapes and sizes; porcelain and enamel are the best choice, as plastic tends to repel water, causing the pools of color to "shrink" as you mix them; **g** jars for water; **h** paper towels, or tissues, and **i** sponges for mopping up spills, or soaking up excess moisture on the painting itself; **j** kneadable eraser; **k** plastic eraser; **l** Q-tips for lifting smaller areas of color and correcting minor mistakes; **m** set square with bevelled edges; **n** clamps for fastening supports to your board; **o** pencil sharpener; **p** craft knife and **q** matt knife for sharpening pencils; **r** a range of graphite pencils (8H, 7H, 6H, 5H, 4H, 3H, 2H, H, HB, F, B, 2B, 3B, 4B, 5B, 6B and 7B); **s** metal ruler; **t** ruler with bevelled edge.

PIGMENTS

THE COLORS USED by artists are made from pigments – powder obtained from the earth, from plants, from minerals, or from animals. The so-called "earth pigments", such as the umbers and siennas, are impure oxides of iron containing manganese oxide, which are dug from the ground. Raw umber is a yellowish brown, and burnt umber is a rich warm brown. The siennas, in general, are yellowish brown, or red – raw sienna is a dull, sandy yellow, and burnt sienna a rich reddish auburn. Another important category consists of the ochres, of which yellow ochre is by far the most popular and useful. The ochres, all yellow or yellowish brown, come mainly from clay containing iron oxide.

The earthy green terre verte originates as an iron silicate. Apart from this natural pigment – and chromium oxide which also produces green – the greens are usually made by mixing the yellow and blue pigments.

Some colors are made from inorganic pigments, such as cadmium yellow, which is produced by the precipitation of cadmium sulphide with zinc sulphide or cadmium selenide, to achieve a pale or deeper tone respectively. (The chemical reaction known as precipitation, "throws out" insoluble material from a solution.) Cadmium red results from the precipitation of cadmium sulphide and selenide. The cadmium yellows and reds, each of which comes in three tones – light, medium and dark – are expensive but, because they are regarded as being the nearest achievable equivalent of primary yellow and red, they are considered to be essential for paints. Colors can also originate from animal and vegetable sources, but modern equivalents devised in the laboratory, are cheaper, and often indistinguishable from the originals.

The older colors

Throughout the history of painting, the number of colors available to the artist has been slowly increasing. The palette of the prehistoric cave painters was limited to comparatively easily

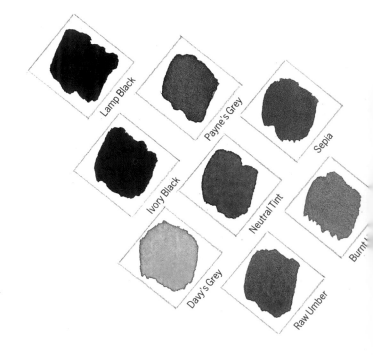

A CHRONOLOGY OF PIGMENTS
Many of the colors in the artist's palette today are made from comparatively modern pigments, which were discovered, or manufactured in the 19th and 20th centuries; others have been known to painters for hundreds of years. Madder and cinnabar, for example, were in use more than 2000 years ago; while viridian, chrome yellow, the cadmiums and the cobalts are among the many newer pigments.

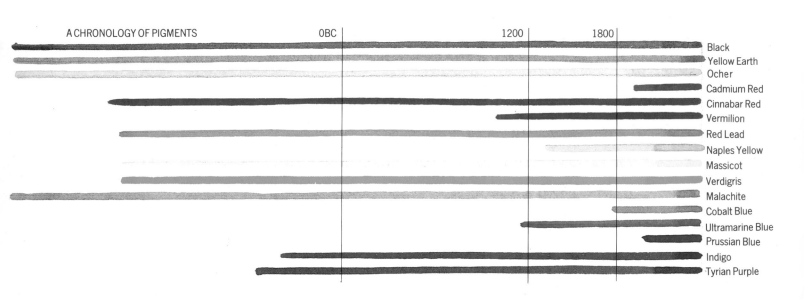

A CHRONOLOGY OF PIGMENTS

	0BC	1200	1800	
				Black
				Yellow Earth
				Ocher
				Cadmium Red
				Cinnabar Red
				Vermilion
				Red Lead
				Naples Yellow
				Massicot
				Verdigris
				Malachite
				Cobalt Blue
				Ultramarine Blue
				Prussian Blue
				Indigo
				Tyrian Purple

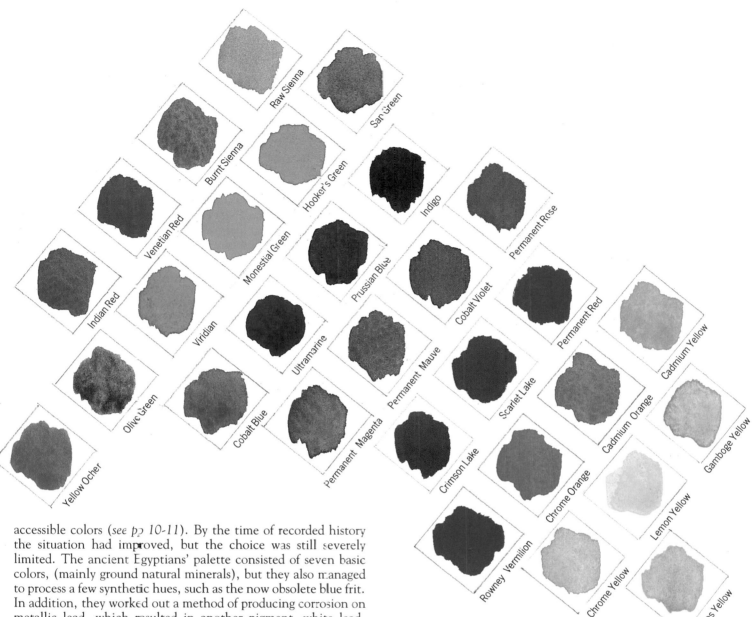

accessible colors (*see pp 10-11*). By the time of recorded history the situation had improved, but the choice was still severely limited. The ancient Egyptians' palette consisted of seven basic colors, (mainly ground natural minerals), but they also managed to process a few synthetic hues, such as the now obsolete blue frit. In addition, they worked out a method of producing corrosion on metallic lead, which resulted in another pigment, white lead. Although this heavy powder is poisonous, the pigment was widely used for centuries – right up to and including the present day. Its traditional "rival" white pigment, chalk, did not have the body or "hiding power" – the ability to cover other colors – of white lead.

The Romans added more colors: from the whelk they made Tyrian purple; verdigris was manufactured by means of a chemical reaction using copper plate; and indigo, a naturally occurring dye obtained from plants, was adapted for use as an artist's paint, as well as a dye for clothes. Modern indigo is synthetically manufactured from aniline, a substance obtained from coal tar.

Three colors which are still widely used and very popular were developed around the 13th century – vermilion, madder and ultramarine; but it was not until the later Middle Ages that the range of colors for the artist was increased to any substantial extent. New hues were added as spin-offs of the cloth-dyeing industry, and of crafts such as glass-making which were gradually growing in sophistication and use of materials.

Some of the colors which are now automatic choices for the artist's palette were not discovered until the 19th century, or later. These include cobalt blue, cadmium red, cadmium yellow and veridian; while two whites, zinc and titanium, have emerged as alternatives to the toxic lead.

COLOR RANGE
There are more than 60 colors potentially available to the watercolor artist; however, the actual range will depend on the individual manufacturer. The 37 colors shown above are among the most popular. Most artists tend to develop particular favorites, usually restricting their palettes to ten or 12 basic hues.

TONES AND NEUTRALS

TONES – THE LIGHTS AND DARKS – contribute as much to a successful painting as the colors themselves. Every color has a tonal value, a shade of gray ranging from almost white to almost black. A pale color, such as yellow, is tonally light; deeper colors, such as red, are tonally dark. If you can imagine how a color would look in a black and white photograph, you are close to understanding its tonal value.

When planning and painting a picture, the tones should be given careful consideration. If you find it difficult to see and assess the tones of your subject, try looking at it through half-closed eyes. This eliminates some of the local color, making it easier for you to pick out its light and dark areas. An awareness of tone, of the contrast between lights and darks, can help you bring a subject to life. If the tones are ignored, your painting will lack a feeling of space; three-dimensional forms, without the proper balance of light and shade to describe them, can look flat or otherwise distorted; and your composition can seem altogether uninspired and visually dull. The arrangement of the lights and darks can be responsible for the success or failure of a painting.

As soon as you begin to tone down a pure primary color, or a pure mix of two primaries, you will start to approach what are known as the neutral colors. These are the hues which are much lower in "saturation", i.e. they have less color-brilliance. As green, for instance, becomes less green, it becomes more neutral, or it begins gradually to approach gray.

The word "pure" is applied to a primary color, or a mix of two primaries. There are various ways of lowering the saturation of these pure hues: you can simply add white, which immediately begins to remove some of the pure color brilliance; thus red becomes less red and more pinkish. (In watercolor painting, of course, you could simply add more water, diluting the color so that more of the white paper shows through.) Another way is to add black, which darkens the colors; although this is rarely advised because it tends to deaden colors. (An alternative would be to add a dark hue, such as raw umber or Payne's gray.)

A third method of lowering the saturation of a "pure mix" of two primaries is to add another color, thus producing a neutral. First, take a single primary color, and mix an equal amount of another primary with it. You have now produced another pure color: red and blue, for instance, make violet. If you add a third color, you will create a duller, less pure hue, which is the neutral. You can adjust the color-bias, i.e. the extent to which one color is more recognizable than the others, by varying the proportions in the mixture.

In practical terms, neutrals are extremely important. If you paint always in pure colors, their impact will be lost and you will produce a rather flat picture, lacking form and interest. Without neutrals, the contrast, which allows the viewer to compare the brightness of a primary or secondary is lost. You also need neutrals to create harmony in a picture: if the neutrals are mixed from the basic colors used in the composition, the final picture will have a synthesis, a sense of wholeness. Another way of achieving this sense of harmony would be to choose a theme color, one which reflects the character of the subject, and to mix a little of this with most of the colors used in the painting.

THE TONAL SCALE
For each color there is a tonal equivalent, somewhere on a scale between very dark gray and very light gray (above left). With watercolor this means that you need mix only one tone – the darkest. Water can then be added to make progressively diluted, and therefore lighter, tones. The still life (above) shows the same subject, first in colors and then in tones.

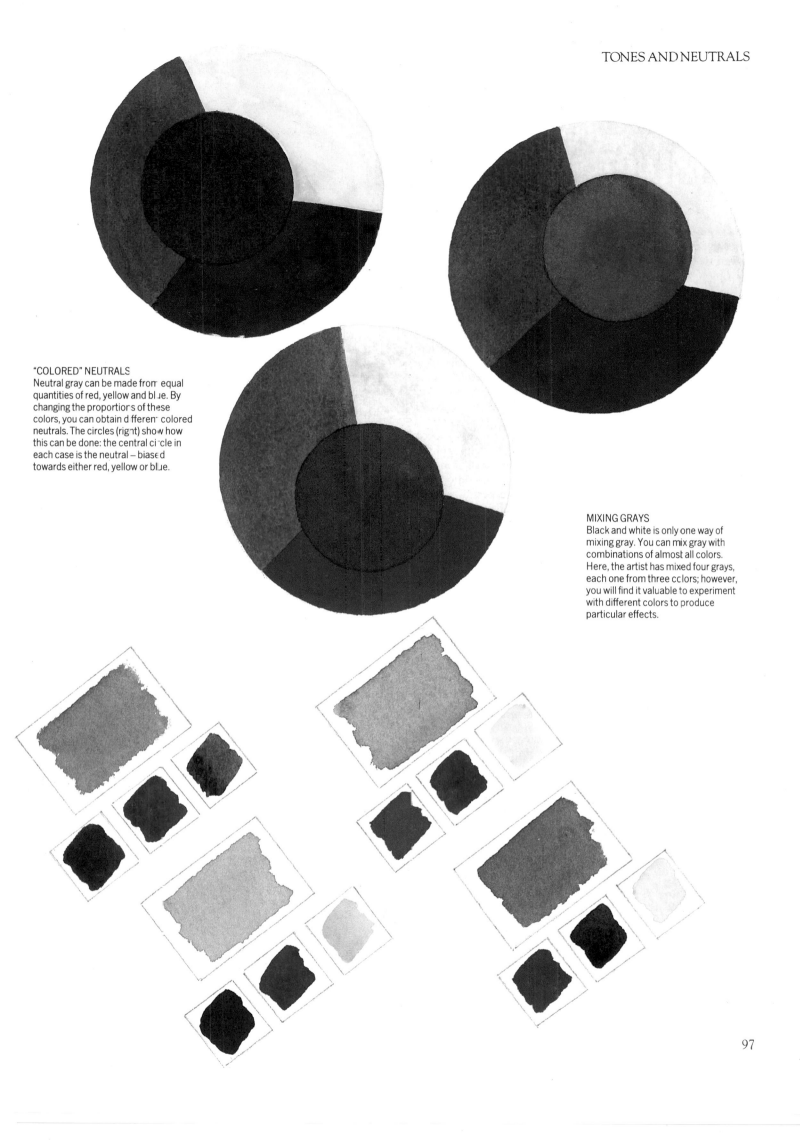

"COLORED" NEUTRALS
Neutral gray can be made from equal quantities of red, yellow and blue. By changing the proportions of these colors, you can obtain different colored neutrals. The circles (right) show how this can be done: the central circle in each case is the neutral – biased towards either red, yellow or blue.

MIXING GRAYS
Black and white is only one way of mixing gray. You can mix gray with combinations of almost all colors. Here, the artist has mixed four grays, each one from three colors; however, you will find it valuable to experiment with different colors to produce particular effects.

DRAWING FOR WATERCOLOR

DRAWING FOR PAINTING is a special category of drawing; it is very different from making a drawing which is intended as an end in itself. One of the differences is that you do not have to think about tone when drawing for a watercolor, as this will be indicated later by the paint; an outline, therefore, is usually sufficient at this stage.

There are various ways of making drawings for watercolor, but the most usual is probably to execute a line drawing in ordinary graphite pencil. An HB or B pencil would be best. If the drawing is too soft, the graphite becomes mixed with the colors, producing a dirty looking painting.

Remember that the lines of the drawing should not be too heavy, otherwise they will show through the paint. In some cases, this might be permissible if you are aiming for a certain effect, but generally it is not desirable. Therefore, if your drawing is too dark, or you find that you have a large number of corrections, rub over it with a putty eraser, until you have a faint, light drawing which is just clear enough to act as a guide for painting in the color.

Colored pencils

Some artists, particularly illustrators, use colored pencils for their initial drawings, often making the outline a darker tone of the local, painted color. On the whole, this produces a decorative rather than a representational effect, but it is well worth experimenting, in order to broaden your visual repertoire. Remember, however, that this method tends to flatten a picture, turning it into a more illustrative image.

Painting direct

Quite often you can work without drawing an outline. If you are painting wet into wet, with loose washes, you can build up the image by imposing areas of tone and color without the use of linear contours. This approach can be employed for any subject, but is particularly appropriate for atmospheric landscapes, skies, clouds, reflections in water, or any other subject which consists of a nebulous mass rather than defined shapes. It can also be useful when you wish to produce a personal impression, an interpretation rather than a strictly representational picture. Caroline

HOW TO START
There are two basic ways of starting a watercolor: you can draw an outline in pen, or pencil; or you can paint directly onto the paper. These diagrams illustrate the varied results produced by different approaches.
a It is best to use a fairly hard pencil, because the graphite will not smudge into the paper, and is light enough not to show through the watercolor.
b Draw the outline in the local color of the subject, so that the line will integrate with the watercolor. **c** If an outline is done in waterproof ink, the watercolor does not dissolve the lines, but leaves them sharp and intact.
d Lines done in water-soluble ink bleed into the wet paint, producing a soft, blended appearance. **e** When color is applied directly, without any preliminary drawing, it produces a loose, washy effect.

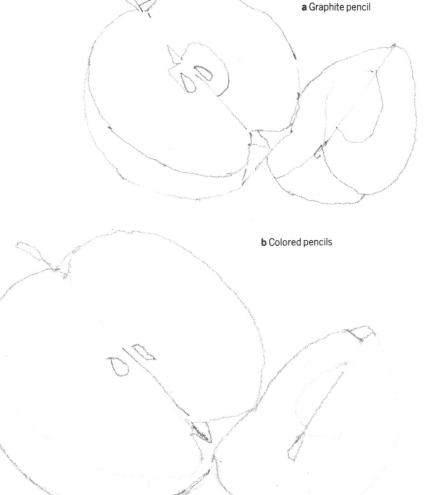

a Graphite pencil

b Colored pencils

Bailey (*see p 73*) uses watercolor in this way. By painting directly onto a damp sheet of paper, she seeks to produce a spontaneous burst of color unrestricted by predetermined outlines.

Pen and wash

Pen and wash is such an established way of working that it is almost regarded as a medium in its own right. There are basically two ways of approaching this technique: you can make a drawing with ink and then wash in the areas of color; or you can start with loose washes of color, and then draw into them with line when the paint is dry. For both methods, the traditional dip pen gives an interesting line, as well as allowing you to control the thickness of the line by pressing harder to make thicker lines, or slanting the nib to make thinner marks. Alternatively, you can use a technical pen (rapidograph) to produce lines of a more regular thickness.

Inks come in various colors, although traditionally black and sepia tones are predominant. The ink can be either waterproof, or water-soluble. If you want the line to remain intact and not bleed into the color, use waterproof ink, but if you want to soften contours, sometimes water-soluble ink can be employed, allowing some bleeding to take place.

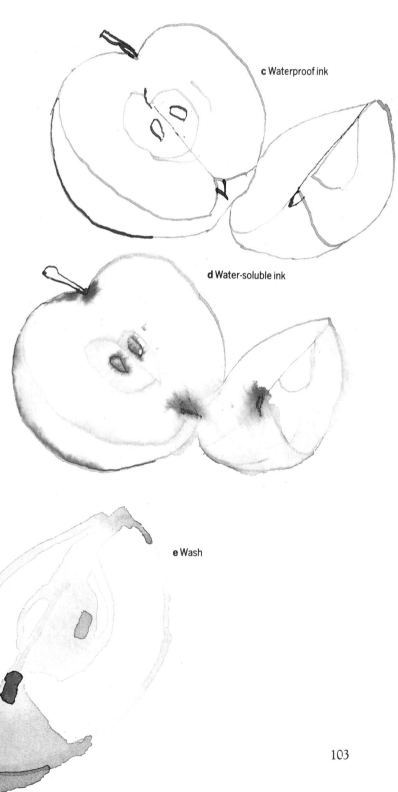

c Waterproof ink

d Water-soluble ink

e Wash

PRACTICAL WATERCOLOR

IT IS NOW TIME to put principles into action. Here, to help you to do this to best effect, the key watercolor principles and techniques are each explained in detail and are followed by a specially-devised step-by-step project or projects, so that you can put what you have learned into practice and see what specific effects the techniques can be used to create. As a result, you will have a wealth of skills at your fingertips. Your visual vocabulary will have been broadened, allowing you to choose the best possible approach — one that not only suits the subject, but also your own personal way of working.

Remember one crucial point. Although the projects have been specifically devised to demonstrate how the various techniques can be best exploited, you should not struggle to follow the instructions to the absolute letter. Watercolor, by its nature, can be an unpredictable medium, so the effects you achieve will never be precisely the same as the ones illustrated here.

Step by step illustrations by Ian Sidaway

STRETCHING PAPER

THE NEED TO stretch your support arises when you wish to use lightweight paper, or when the picture you have in mind involves a series of very wet washes. In both cases, unstretched paper will tend to buckle (*see pp 84-5*).

For stretching paper, you will need a suitable board: it has to be smooth, to avoid affecting the surface of the paper, and must be thick enough not to warp when wet, or when the paper contracts. Thin plywood is not suitable – you need a stable drawing board, or a piece of laminated wood.

You can use either gummed paper, or staples to secure the paper to the board.

USING GUMMED TAPE

1. Cut strips of brown gummed tape to fit the edges of your paper.

2. Wet the paper, either by using a sponge, or by immersing it in water.

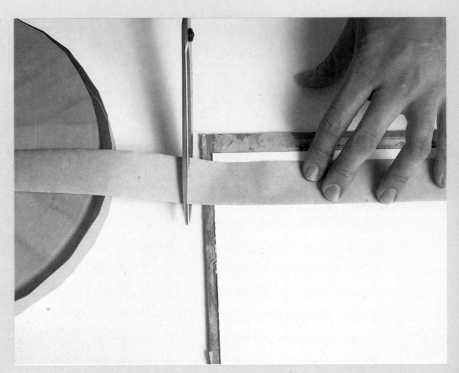

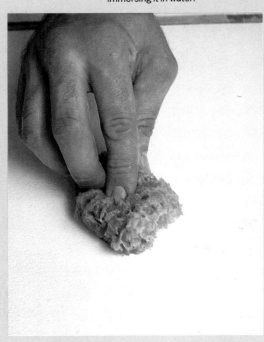

3. Lay the paper flat on the board, sized side up. Remove any air bubbles by rubbing briskly outwards from the center with a clean cloth, and then stick down the edges with the strips of gummed tape. Allow the paper to dry naturally.

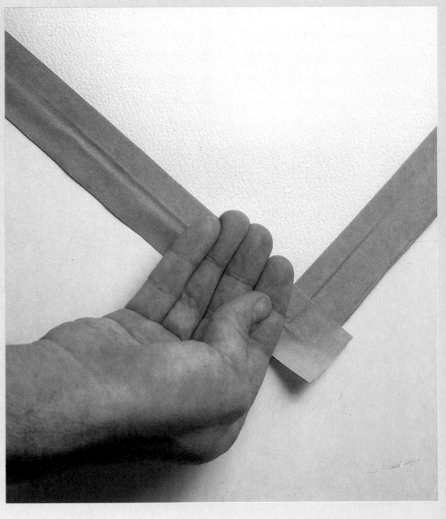

USING STAPLES

1. This method is suitable for heavy watercolor papers. Place the paper over the board and fold down the edges. Cut the corners to fit.

2. Fold the corners neatly, and press them down. Now, staple the sides of the paper to the board.

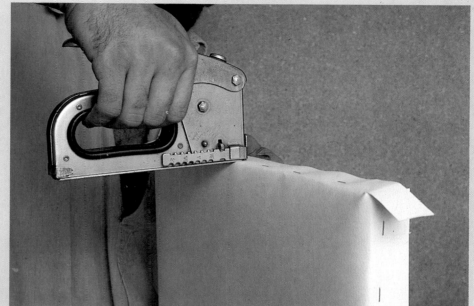

3. Staple the corners down. Finally, wet the surface of the paper with a sponge, and allow it to dry.

MIXING PAINT

WHEN MIXING WATERCOLOR paint you have to aim not only at achieving the right color, but also the correct consistency. The latter is all-important if you want to control the tones and colors, for this transparent medium is built up in several layers.

If you know you will be working in two or three tones of the same color, it is often a good idea to mix these in advance. Whether you are using pans, cakes or tubes, the mixing is a matter of patient trial and error. You cannot tell by looking at the paint on the palette whether you have achieved the right consistency: the color must be seen on paper. Therefore, when mixing, you should always have a piece of spare paper at hand for testing the colors.

With cakes or pans, moisten the paint and work the color with a brush to release the pigment. Cakes are particularly dry and absorbent so this can take quite a long time. Then, transfer some of this color to your palette, or mixing dish to be mixed with other colors according to your requirements. When using tubes, squeeze a small quantity of the paint directly onto the palette; then pick up a little of the color on the brush, transfer this to the mixing dish, and gradually add the water, drop by drop. For very pale washes, you need only one or two spots of color, diluted with a large amount of water.

Once you have achieved a particular color, the only way you will be able to re-mix it is by trial and error; so, whenever possible, start by mixing color you will need.

Gouache

The consistency of gouache does not greatly affect the overall color, which makes it easier to mix than watercolor. If you use a large amount of water with gouache, you can produce a wash-like effect, but this is never as transparent as pure watercolor.

When mixing gouache to a particular consistency, therefore, you are usually concerned not so much with time, but with how you will use the paint: for example, when masking, the paint should be fairly thick and creamy; while for spattering, it should be comparatively thin.

Gouache dries darker than it appears when it is wet. This means it is important to test the color first on a piece of paper, allowing it to dry, before applying paint to the actual picture.

WATERCOLOR
1. Using porcelain or enamel mixing dishes, mix the water and paint to the required strength. For small quantities of normal, or strong color, start with the paint and add water drop by drop from the brush. For pale washes, you can add the paint to the water.

2. Mix enough of each color to complete the task. If you run out of a particular mixed color, you will find it difficult to re-mix the exact tone.

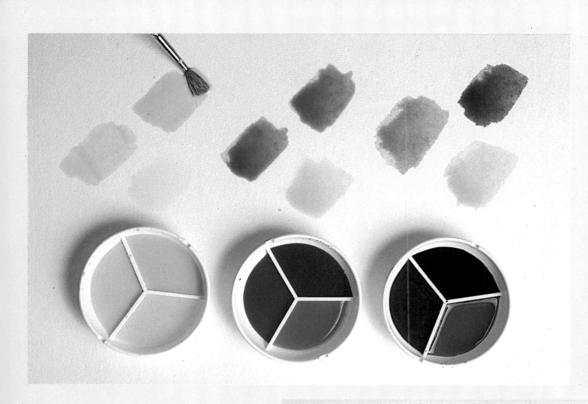

3. Test the color on white paper to see if you have mixed the correct strength of hue.

GOUACHE

1. Choose the colors you think will achieve a particular hue. Mix together a small quantity of each color, and adjust the hue by adding more color. Finally, add water until the paint reaches the required thickness.

2. Gouache, particularly mixed colors usually dries darker than it appears when wet. It is essential therefore, to test each color on white paper, and then allow it to dry before using it on the actual picture.

WET ON DRY

WET ON DRY is the expression used to describe the process of painting watercolor onto a dry surface. It is the main, classical method of using watercolors, and includes anything from broad washes applied with a large brush, to adding the tiniest detail. Darker and darker tones are built up by putting one thin layer of color on top of another; each layer is allowed to dry before the next one is added.

Wet on dry washes can be applied as areas of flat color, as illustrated; alternatively, they can be graded by diluting, or strengthening the paint to make the color lighter or darker as you move down the paper. When painting broad washes, it is important to keep the color moving, and not to let the paint dry between strokes, as this can cause streaks and tidemarks.

The wet on dry method is ideal for precise illustration work: the dry surface "holds" the paint, so that smaller shapes and specific details will not blob or distort. However, this method does not necessarily restrict you to painting shapes with hard, crisp edges: for example, if you are painting a rounded form, you could depict the tones in specific shapes, and then use water to blend them together. Neither does painting wet on dry prevent you from achieving hazy, or atmospheric effects; again, colors can be merged by applying water.

LAYING WET ON DRY

1. Slightly tilt the board. Then, load a wash brush with a diluted color, and begin by painting a band across the top of the support. Work from side to side, spreading the color evenly, and painting quickly to prevent the edge of the color from drying.

2. When you reach the bottom of the support, set the board flat and allow the color to dry.

PAINTING WET ON DRY

1. To paint wet on dry, allow the first layer of color to dry thoroughly before painting over it.

2. The new color retains its shape, and dries with clean crisp edges.

A SEASCAPE

THIS VIEW OF a dramatic outcrop of black and white stratified rocks jutting into the sea was painted with a series of "wet into dry" washes.

By allowing the paint to dry after each wash was applied, in typical "wet into dry" manner, the artist was able to lay the color in clean, graphic shapes and to use the texture and character of the brushstrokes as a positive feature of the painting. (The strokes are held instantly by the dry surface, instead of blending and running together as they would on wet paper.) For instance, when painting the later stages of the water, he worked with an irregular flicking movement, using the strokes to capture the broken, undulating texture of the sea.

Working in the traditional watercolor method of building up color, the artist applied layer after layer of consecutive thin washes to create increasingly darker tones, and used the lightness of the paper to represent white areas and highlights. The white base color of the rocks is simply the white surface of the paper.

Without their seascape context, the rocks themselves would be less interesting. It is the watery void around them which gives the rocks their character, emphasizing the jagged outlines and angular contours. The artist has exploited this contrast in the textures of the rocks and water by deliberately placing the subject in an asymmetrical composition. Divided diagonally by the rocks themselves, the painting is split into two definite halves, the task of the top one being to draw the viewer's attention to the rocks.

WATERCOLOR PALETTE	
Payne's Gray	Chinese White
Yellow Ochre	Alizarin Crimson
Ivory Black	Cadmium Orange
Raw Umber	
SUPPORT	
Stretched cartridge paper	

1. PENCIL OUTLINE
First draw a faint but sharp outline of the rocks and lighthouse, using an H pencil. The lines should be definite enough to act as a clear guide for the ensuing colors, but not so dark that they will show through.

2. FIRST WASH
Working onto dry, stretched paper (see pp 84-5), apply an extremely diluted wash of Payne's gray mixed with a touch of yellow ochre, so that it covers the entire area of sea and sky. Use a No. 6 sable wash brush, changing to a No. 4 sable round brush for the precise work around the edges of the initial outline.

3. DARKER WASH
Leave the wash to dry (the artist speeded this up with a hair-dryer); then, using the same color, but less diluted, work in a second wash with horizontal strokes, leaving small fragments of the underwash to show through.

4. BASE OF ROCKS
Use a very diluted mixture of ivory black and yellow ochre, and a No. 2 round sable brush to put down the first layer of the dark stratum around the base of the rocks. Keep the layer simple, with no detail, as this will be built up later.

5. DARKER BASE
Use a darker tone of the same color around the base of the rock formation to indicate the shadows, crevices and outlines of the rock itself. This is the only time the artist moved away slightly from the wet into dry routine: to avoid harsh lines, he applied the darker color before the base had quite dried.

6. SHADOWS
Deepen the shadows cast by the rocks with the original, No. 6, wash brush. There is a simple but effective way of representing the varied directions of the waves. Using Payne's gray, make slightly crisscrossed strokes, interlocking them in places. Leave patches of under-wash showing, as this will give the impression of light reflecting on the moving water.

7. ROCK DETAILS

Use a No. 2 round sable brush for this next stage. Squeeze the moisture out of the brush until it is almost dry to pick up the color; lightly drag the Payne's gray and yellow ochre sea-mixture across the surface of the rocks, so that the direction of the lines will imitate the chipped, flint-like strata.

8. LIGHTHOUSE

Use a mixture of alizarin crimson and cadmium orange for the red band and top of the lighthouse. First apply a flat, thinnish layer of the color; then follow it with a deeper version of the same color. Leave a small section of the first layer showing; the paler color will indicate reflected light and show the rounded form of the building. Both these steps should be done with the smaller No. 2 brush, ensuring that this part of the picture — the focal point — is tight and precise compared with the wide, loose washes that surround it.

9. FINISHING TOUCHES

With part of the lighthouse now in shade, you can use a light wash to develop the form. Mix the shadow wash for the red areas from cadmium orange and black, and the wash for the white areas from raw umber and ivory black. Next, touch in the windows with ivory black. Tonal adjustments can be made by introducing a little Payne's gray and yellow ochre sea-color into the dark base areas of the rocks.

You can now add the final touch. To portray the white foam in the water lapping around the rocks, use a No. 2 brush coated in Chinese white and roll the brush on the surface of the water. However, do not become too enthusiastic because, if the effect is overdone, the result will lose credibility.

WET ON WET

PAINTING WET ON WET is used less frequently than the more classical wet on dry approach. You paint onto a damp surface, applying the paint either to paper which has been moistened, or laying one color on top of another which has not yet dried. It is the way in which some watercolor painters achieve a sense of spontaneity, for the results can never be exactly anticipated. The element of surprise is the reason why, after practice and experience, many painters find this method an exciting and challenging one.

A wet on wet wash involves dampening the paper with a large brush, or a sponge, and then applying color in broad, horizontal strokes. It takes practice to do this successfully, as it is not always easy to achieve a flat color.

When you paint a color onto another wet color, the two run into each other. This means you cannot work in the traditional light to dark manner because the colors do not remain separate. Caroline Bailey's work is a good example of the effects which can be achieved with this method. Her loosely painted flowers are the result of a very spontaneous, free approach (*see p 73*).

Working with wet on wet, you will never have complete control over the final effect. However, if you allow the under-layer of color to dry partially before adding more colors, they will blend without running amok, and you will be able to plan the result to some extent.

LAYING A WET ON WET WASH
1. Working on stretched paper, and using a natural sponge, wet the surface with clean water. Then, slightly tilt the board, and apply the color in horizontal stripes from top to bottom.

2. This technique takes practice. There is less risk of tidemarks than when laying a wet on dry wash, but you will occasionally see tonal changes in the horizontal stripes.

PAINTING WET ON WET

1. Allow the first color to partially dry — it should be damp rather than wet. Then apply your second color.

2. The paint spreads slightly, leaving a soft shape with a slightly blurred edge.

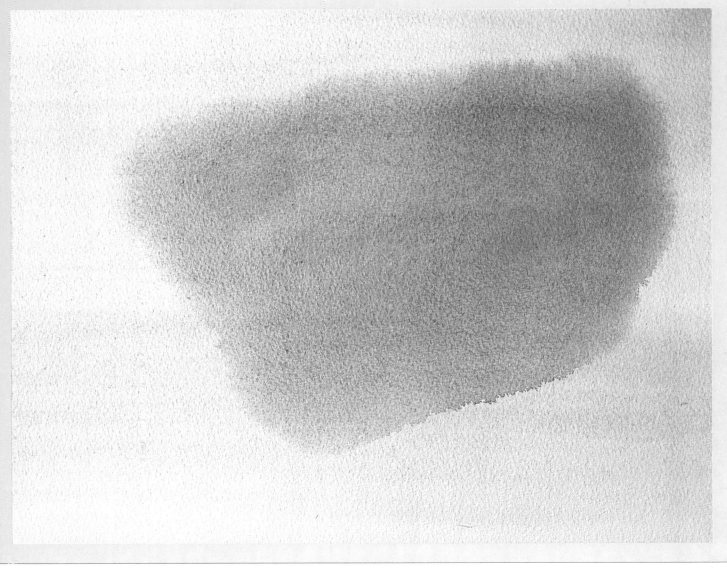

BASKET OF FRUIT

THE TECHNIQUE OF painting wet on wet has been used primarily to establish the main shapes of the image, and to help create color harmony. The artist laid each color without waiting for the previous one to dry, which meant that the paint ran, causing the colors to merge in a softly blended edge.

This method can be especially effective for still-life arrangements of fruit because the colors – typically reds, greens, yellows and oranges – are related. Each fruit has elements of all the other colors in it; thus, when they are painted, the red in the peppers can be allowed to blend into the green apples, the green pepper has patches of warm red in it, and so on. This rather loose, splashy beginning therefore acts as a unifying base for further development, as well as being ideal for blending colors on natural forms, and suggesting the rounded characteristics of the fruit. Nowhere are there any harsh divisions of tone or color.

Wet on wet is not suited to tightly painted detail; however, the artist felt it was important to depict the wicker weave of the basket, as this would bring the whole subject into sharper focus, and help it to hold its own against the dramatic background tone. He therefore abandoned his wet on wet technique, to paint the dark wicker pattern onto dry color, in crisp calligraphic brushmarks.

WATERCOLOR PALETTE	
Cadmium Orange	Yellow Ochre
Raw Umber	Cadmium Green
Cadmium Red	Cadmium Yellow
Sap Green	Sepia
Lemon Yellow	Indigo
Black	
SUPPORT	
Bockingford paper, stretched 660 × 457mm (26 × 18in)	

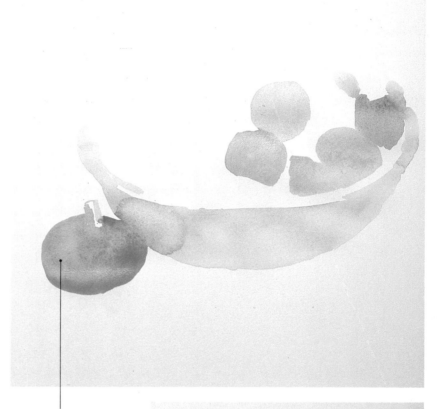

1. FIRST STAGE
Painting directly onto the paper, and without first making a pencil drawing of the subject, start immediately to block in the main areas of color. Use a wash brush to paint the oranges and pumpkin in cadmium orange; the apple and pepper in cadmium green; and the basket in yellow ochre mixed with raw umber. Keep the color fairly thin at this stage, so that you can add darker tones later.

2. MORE FRUIT
Continue to block in the fruit and vegetables in flat shapes of thin wash. Work quickly, without waiting for the paint to dry between colors. Where it is desirable to keep the colors separate, leave an area of white space between the shapes; otherwise, allow the wet colors to run into each other. For example, the artist has allowed the greens, yellows and oranges to merge, and has incorporated these "accidental" effects. Add shadows to the basket and the table in a diluted mixture of sepia and black.

3. TWO-COLOR SURFACES

Exploit the wet on wet method to depict fruit and vegetables with two, or more surface colors: the pepper, for instance, is red and green; therefore, the artist has painted cadmium red onto wet sap green to achieve a natural-looking effect.

4. DETAILS

Change to a No. 2 brush when developing the details on the fruit and vegetables. You should aim, wherever possible, to describe the forms and surface textures: for example, the dark orange markings on the pumpkin help to depict its rounded form.

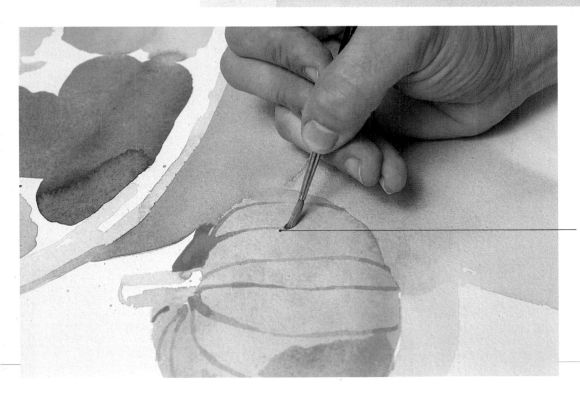

5. MORE DETAIL
Work into the grapes with sap green; and develop the glossy surface of the pepper with more red and green, applied wet on wet. Add darker tones of cadmium orange to the pumpkin, without flattening the effect of the linear markings.

6. DARKER TONES
Work into the darker tones of the subject and, by strengthening the colors, bring out the individual shapes and characteristics of the fruits and vegetables. Now, darken the shadows on the basket to match these newly established, stronger colors and tones. Paint the tabletop with a pale sepia wash.

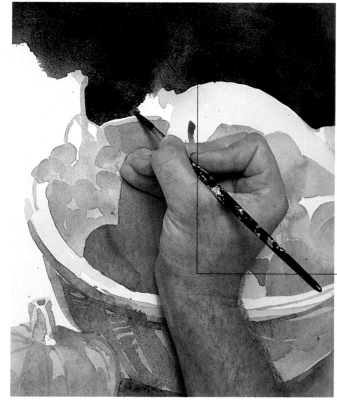

7. BACKGROUND
Block in the background with dark blue. The artist felt that the actual background was too close in tone and color to the subject, so he chose a mixture of indigo and black, which emphasizes the contrasting colors of the fruit and vegetables. Allow the background to dry before going on to the next stage.

8. BASKET DETAIL
Develop the weave of the basket with black diagonal lines. This dark pattern gives the basket shape and emphasis; and because the black lines are the same strength of tone as the deep blue background, they help the subject to stand out from the surrounding tone, instead of being overwhelmed by it.

9. ADJUSTMENTS
Working with a wash brush, and using the broad, free approach of the early steps, make any necessary alterations to the colors and tones. Here, the artist took the opportunity to darken and redefine the pepper, apple and bananas.

10. FINISHING TOUCHES
Finally, the artist worked across the picture, pinpointing the deepest shadows with black and indigo. By extending the background color into every part of the image he brought the separate elements together, and integrated the composition.

PEN AND WASH

YOU CAN COMBINE line with watercolor in a very fluid and sympathetic way by using the pen and wash technique – a traditional combination which has been employed for hundreds of years, and was especially popular with the English painters of the 18th century. The method is still a favorite, particularly with illustrators.

Pen and wash allows the artist either to draw the subject first and then add colors, or to block in the image with loose washes of color, and then to define the image and add details with line. By using an old-fashioned dip pen, the artist can obtain a varied and fluid line, which is particularly in keeping with the watercolor medium. Many artists, including such masters as Thomas Rowlandson (*see p 37*) and Rubens (*see pp 22-3*), worked in this way. Black or sepia were the traditional colors for pen and wash, but ·modern painters and illustrators employ the full range of colors.

Waterproof, or water-soluble inks can be used, depending upon whether you wish to achieve a hard, or a blended line. You can also indicate tone with a pen, by hatching, or cross-hatching the shadows and dark areas with the nib, and using paint for the local color, as shown here.

LINE ON DRY PAPER
1. Take a dip pen and start to build up the tone in patches of short parallel lines. The darker the tone you wish to achieve, the closer the lines should be, and the more you will need to overlay the shading.

3. The water has blurred the lines, giving the impression of a watercolor wash.

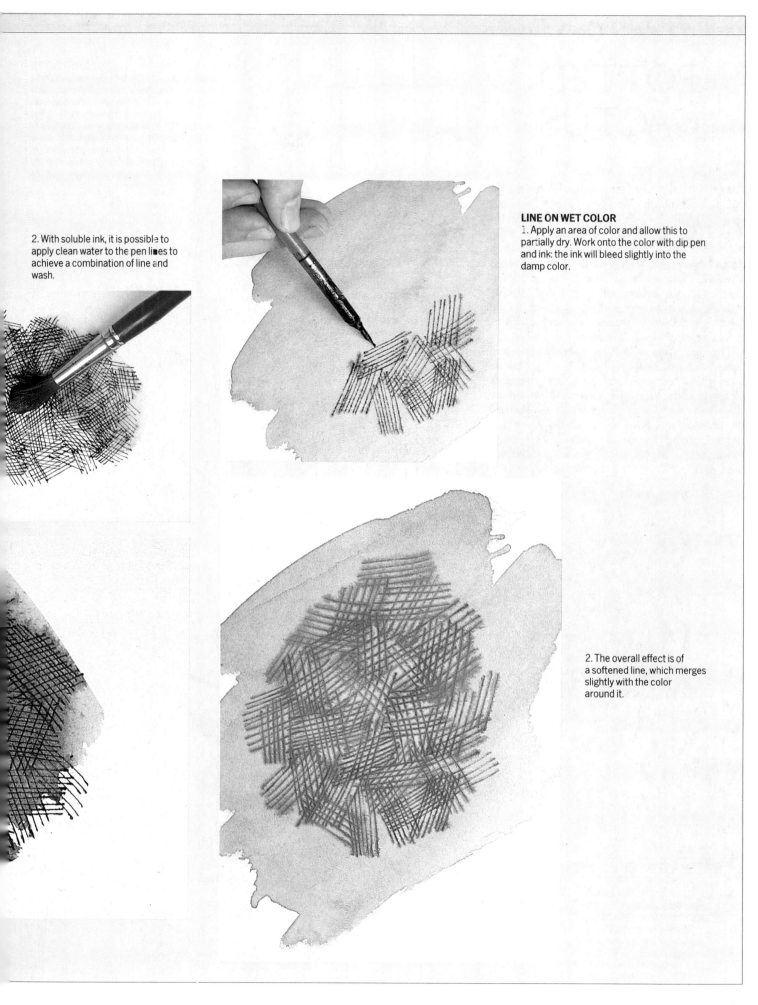

2. With soluble ink, it is possible to apply clean water to the pen lines to achieve a combination of line and wash.

LINE ON WET COLOR
1. Apply an area of color and allow this to partially dry. Work onto the color with dip pen and ink: the ink will bleed slightly into the damp color.

2. The overall effect is of a softened line, which merges slightly with the color around it.

7. BLENDING COLORS
Quickly wash a little clean water across the stonework on the church, blending the colors slightly, but taking care not to lose them completely. Redefine some of the individual stones, with pen lines.

8. BACKGROUND TREES
Paint the background trees in sap green and Payne's gray, making the farthest row paler to indicate distance (see pp134-5).

9. STRENGTHENING TONES
Work across the painting, strengthening tones, and developing detail. Here, the artist uses bold black to emphasize the window recess.

10. FINISHING TOUCHES
A variety of materials and marks bring a lively, graphic quality to the completed picture; while the warmly-toned paper holds the separate elements and unrelated colors together. Thus, despite a free and uninhibited approach, the image retains a strong sense of unity

THE TUILERIES, PARIS

IN THIS SPACIOUS study, the artist has made use of linear and aerial perspective to create a sense of space and distance. The eye is arrested immediately by the three stone urns standing in a stately row, which take the viewer right to the back of the composition.

The square bases of the urns have the same vanishing point – and here a word of warning is necessary. If you are going to make use of something as obvious and stark as this to give your composition perspective, then you must make absolutely sure you render it correctly. If not, the result shows up as a glaring mistake, so the time spent plotting out the vanishing point and receding lines is well invested. If you cannot do this by eye, it is a good idea to construct it formally with a ruler.

Aerial perspective reinforces the sense of distance. The colors and tones, and therefore the shapes, of the objects in the distance are much fainter and fade into a similarity of tone – all of which creates atmosphere. As well as having its strict vanishing point, the row of urns is also given this aerial perspective. The distant urns become lighter and less defined.

The stone urn in the foreground, however, really jumps out at the viewer, adding to the illusion of distance existing behind it. The artist has deliberately ignored the local color to concentrate on the contrast between the light and dark of the carved stonework. The urn has a "printed" quality of white and dark gray, with almost no tones in between – although some sense of tone has been suggested in places by using dark color on a drybrush.

WATERCOLOR PALETTE	
Cobalt Blue	Sepia
Brown Madder Alizarin	Ivory Black
Payne's Gray	Sap Green
Yellow Ochre	Lemon Yellow

SUPPORT
Bockingford paper, stretched
356 × 508mm (14 × 20in)

1. THE PRELIMINARIES
Make a drawing of the scene, paying particular attention to the perspective of the row of urns – make sure the vanishing point for all three is in the same place. When you are satisfied with the drawing, paint diluted cobalt blue across the sky area with a wash brush. When this is dry, use a smaller brush to block in the lightest tone on the distant building in sepia and brown madder alizarin. Extend this color into the foreground. Leave to dry.

2. WORKING ON THE PALACE
It helps if you use just two basic tones for the main part of the building – the first light wash, and a second deeper tone of sepia, brown madder and a little black. Use the second color for the darker architectural details and the row of trees. Then paint the roof with the same mixture, adding some Payne's gray.

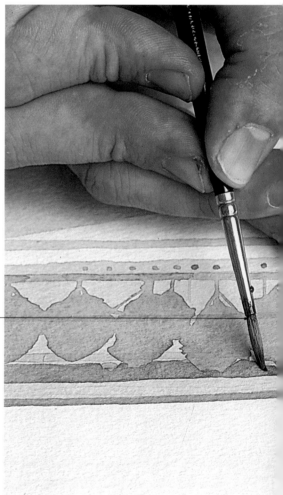

3. DISTANCE AND SPACE
So far, the tones are very pale. In line with the principles of aerial perspective, this is to emphasize distance and space. For the same reason, no clear details are depicted on the far-away objects.

4. URN SHADOWS
Mix some of the warm tones used so far with more Payne's gray, and use this to pick out the shadows on the two distant urns. Leave the highlights as crisp white shapes. Then, with a darker mixture of the same color, paint the shadows of the foreground urn. Again, allow the paper to represent the highlights, but now pick out more of the detail of the carved stonework.

5. DRYBRUSH
Use the drybrush technique to create the pitted, textural surface of the stonework. Do this by squeezing excess moisture from the brush, dipping the ends of the almost-dry bristles in the paint and "scrubbing" the color onto the paper.

6. GRASS AND FOLIAGE
Paint the grass with a mixture of sap green, yellow ochre and lemon yellow. Then, with a very diluted version of the color used earlier for the urns, block in the foliage behind them to provide a solid background for the trees. Leave to dry.

7. GROUND AND TREES
Develop the shadows on the ground, using loosely applied wash and some drybrush to create the gritty, textural surface. Then, with a diluted mixture of Payne's gray and a little yellow ochre, work with a fine brush to "draw in" the first tone of the bare trees.

8. PERSPECTIVE
With a deeper version of the Payne's gray and yellow ochre mixture, paint over the foreground tree shapes. By developing and darkening the objects in the foreground, you are again creating aerial perspective and space in your painting.

9. FINISHING TOUCHES
Complete the picture by working across the image, carefully bringing up the tones to match the new dark shapes of the trees. You may want to darken the tones of the urns, for instance, as this will emphasize the contrast between the light and dark areas, as well as slightly darkening the shadows.

RECEDING HILLS

THIS QUICK WATERCOLOR sketch of green fields and rolling hills that fade stage by stage into the distance, is a perfect example of aerial, or atmospheric perspective. The artist has used two basic principles.

First, he has created distance by making the hills bluer and lighter as they recede. The shading depicts the varying amount of atmosphere between the viewer and the hills – the hazier and bluer the scenery, the farther away it seems – and this automatically creates a sense of distance. On the other hand, the use of specific local color can make scenery appear closer. Hence, the bright green fields are obviously in front of the blue background hills.

The second technique used by the artist involves another basic principle of color theory: cool colors tend to recede, and warm colors tend to come forward. This picture is worked in shades of basic green, which is commonly thought to be a cold color; but this particular green, mixed from sap green and yellows, is warm compared with the cold blue used for the distant features.

When you are building up ranges of distant hills in this way, it is important to allow each layer to dry completely before painting the next one. If you do not, one range of hills will merge into the next, which tends to pull them onto the same plane, instead of establishing a sense of space between them.

WATERCOLOR PALETTE	
Payne's Gray	Cobalt Blue
Sap Green	Lemon Yellow
Yellow Ochre	Sepia
SUPPORT	
Bockingford paper, stretched 508 × 356mm (20 × 14in)	

1. FARTHEST HILLS
Mix a very diluted wash of Payne's gray and cobalt blue and, using a large wash brush, paint the farthest range of hills as a broad stripe of color. This wash is the palest tone in the composition, so it is important to get it right; if the first tone is too deep, the whole painting will be too dark.

2. SECOND RANGE
Allow the first color to dry completely. Now, taking a deeper version of the Payne's gray and cobalt blue mix, paint in the second range of hills: those immediately in front of the ones you have just painted. Allow the paint to dry.

The upper outlines of the hills should be crisp and natural looking. This is easier to achieve if you paint the horizon lines in one stroke, resisting the temptation to go back and re-work them.

3. THIRD RANGE
For the next range of hills, add a little sap green to the basic mixture. Apply this with the wash brush, following the contours of the hill. Allow one or two narrow patches of the lighter undercolor to show through to represent sunlight. Let the paint dry completely.

4. MIDDLE DISTANCE
Introduce more local color into the fields in the middle distance. Use sap green and lemon yellow for the darker green; yellow ochre and lemon yellow for the lighter one. Do not worry if the tone of the fields appears lighter than that of the distant hills; the brighter, warmer colors create an illusion of nearness.

5. FIELDS
Develop the pattern of the fields, using Payne's gray with sap green to dab in the shapes of the trees and hedges with a No. 7 round sable brush. Avoid painting sharp detail, as this contradicts the illusion of distance and tends to bring the subject into the foreground. Instead, use the shape of the brushmarks to give a general impression of foliage and trees.

6. FOREGROUND
With loose brushstrokes, lay in the foreground with a mixture of Payne's gray, sap green and sepia (sepia makes the color warmer).

7. FINISHING TOUCHES
Suggest foliage, twigs and texture by flicking shapes across the damp foreground colors. This slightly defined detail causes the foreground to "jump" forward, thus establishing a sense of space between the distant hills and the foreground area.

ANEMONES IN A WINDOW

ANEMONES ARE NATURALLY bright, colorful flowers, but, because these stand in front of a window, they are thrown almost into silhouette. As a result, the colors are subdued, and both the flowers and the white jug are darker that they would otherwise appear.

Flowers, because of their detail and subtlety of color and structure, are notoriously daunting as a subject for beginners. However, in this project the problem has been substantially simplified: the petals are established in two tones of the same color – a light underpainting and a darker version of the same color to depict simplified shadows. The basic technique is still the classic one of light to dark, even though the color range is simple, and the tones are restricted and relatively dark.

The foliage is actually painted in one color, as flat shapes; but because the lines are fluid and the shapes of the leaves have been faithfully observed, the artist has come close to creating an illusion of real foliage. This effect is enhanced by the fact that where the leaves overlap the color has flooded, creating barely perceptible areas of light and dark.

The artist decided to leave out the background of treetops, because he thought it would detract from the simple effectiveness of the sharply defined flowers and leaves. A few strokes of blue wash were all that was needed to suggest the sky beyond the window, and establish a sense of a larger world outside the room.

WATERCOLOR PALETTE	
Alizarin Crimson	Ivory Black
Brown Madder	Violet Alizarin
Ultramarine Blue	Payne's Gray
Sap Green	Yellow Ochre
SUPPORT	
Saunders paper, stretched 737 × 508mm (29 × 20in)	

1. FIRST STAGE
Working on stretched paper, make a fairly detailed outline of the subject with an HB pencil. Concentrate on the main shapes and on positioning the subject, rather than on detail. Block in the shapes of the flower heads, using a diluted mixture of alizarin crimson and brown madder for the pink anemones, and adding a little ultramarine for the blue flowers.

2. FOLIAGE
Paint the stems and leaves in a fairly flat mixture of sap green and black, with the tip of a No. 2 sable brush. Work quickly to keep the lines free and fluid. You will find this much easier if you hold the brush in a relaxed manner.

3. FLOWER DETAILS
When the first wash is dry, paint in the black anemone centers. Work into the flowers, painting in the petal shadows – sap green and violet alizarin on the blue flowers; sap green and alizarin crimson on the pink.

4. PAINTING THE JUG
Using a No. 7 sable brush, block in the shadows and the reflections on the jug, with a mixture of black, Payne's gray and yellow ochre. Paint the lighter side of the jug with diluted yellow ochre while the shadow areas are still partially wet, allowing the damp colors to merge and produce the rounded, reflective character of the jug.

5. SHADOWS
When the jug is dry, go over the shadows with bold, vertical strokes of the same color to emphasize the roundness. Paint the handle in the same dark tone. Now, return to the flowers, darkening and strengthening the shadow tones on the petals to match the newly established shadows on the jug. Use a large squirrel brush, or a No. 18 wash brush, to paint in the broad areas of the window and sill with a diluted mixture of Payne's gray and yellow ochre.

6. WINDOW SLATS
Make sure the flowers are completely dry, before using the wash brush to paint the window slats in the same basic "window" mix of Payne's gray and yellow ochre. Work quickly, painting with confident, straight strokes, and taking the wash over any leaves and flowers which are in front of the slats.

7. THE FRAME
When the color on the windows is completely dry, use a ruler to paint the mouldings on the frame in a darker mixture of Payne's gray and yellow ochre. Block in the bottom ledge in the same color.

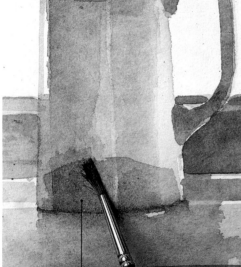

8. FINISHING THE JUG
Darken and develop the tones on the jug. Leaving the white highlights intact, work yellow ochre and Payne's gray into the shadow areas to emphasize the jug's form and shiny surface.

9. DARK TONES
Darken and strengthen the tones on the surrounding window frames to match those of the subject. Use a deep version of the Payne's gray and yellow ochre mixture to emphasize the silhouette effect of the frame.

10. THE SKY
Finally, wash in the sky with diluted cobalt blue, using a wash brush and plenty of clean water to spread the color across the top half of the window area Take the color over the window bars, but do this quickly so as not to disturb the underlying color.

ALEXA

THE LITTLE GIRL'S impish smile, curly hair, and denim clothes are all captured in a portrait which follows the traditional classic watercolor technique: working from light to dark. In this case, the technique is particularly useful because the subject is bathed in golden sunlight and, by giving the whole figure a very pale yellow underpainting, the artist created a base on which to build up local colors and deeper tones. As the painting progressed this pale yellow was allowed to show through in places to represent the warm sunlit areas on the figure.

The portrait looks complicated and filled with lively detail, yet the artist has used a simple device to achieve this effect: each color is reduced to three or four basic tones. The hair, for example, is painted in light brown, mid-brown and a blackish brown; while the face is depicted in a range of three or four tones of a basic flesh color; and the overalls are simplified in terms of light blue, medium blue and dark blue. This comparatively simple approach is so effective in creating a convincing and realistic image that the artist was able to keep the flat white background and still retain a feeling of solid form and surrounding space.

WATERCOLOR PALETTE	
Cadmium Yellow	Brown Madder Alizarin
Raw Umber	Alizarin Crimson
Ivory Black	Ultramarine
Sepia	
SUPPORT	
Bockingford paper, stretched 559 × 406mm (22 × 16in)	

1. FIRST STAGE
Make a drawing of the subject using a fairly hard pencil. The lines should be light, acting as an accurate, though minimal, guide for your watercolors. Mix a very light wash of cadmium yellow, and paint this over the whole subject with a No. 12 sable brush. Let the paint dry.

Paint the next lightest tone into the hair with a No. 4 sable brush. Treat the strands of hair as flat shapes, leaving the pale yellow highlight areas untouched. Allow this to dry, then work a slightly deeper version of the same color into the darker, shaded areas. Again, allow the paint to dry.

2. DARK TONES
Mix black and sepia for the darkest hair tone. Look carefully at the effect of the sunlight falling on one side of the subject, and use this deep tone to pick out the resulting sharp shadows down the darkest side of the head.

3. FLESH TONES
When the hair is completely dry, paint the lightest shadow on the face in a diluted mixture of cadmium yellow, ivory black, sepia and brown madder. Soften the harsh outline of the bangs shadow with a clean brush and a little water, until it blends with the flesh tones.

4. SHADOWS
Paint the dark shadows on the neck and shoulder with a mixture of brown madder, raw umber and ivory black. Add a little gum water to the paint before applying it. The gum water does not affect the color or texture of the watercolor, but it causes subsequent colors to "bleed" and blend into this initial layer of paint, thus avoiding hard, unnatural edges.

5. CLOTHING
Progress to the girl's clothing, and block in the overalls with a diluted mixture of black and ultramarine blue. As before, paint the lightest area first, and then build up progressively darker shadows.

6. STRONGER TONES
Once some of the basic tones have been established, you can work across the painting, sharpening and strengthening those areas which, in relation to the whole figure, now look too pale. Here, some of the hair shadows are being redefined.

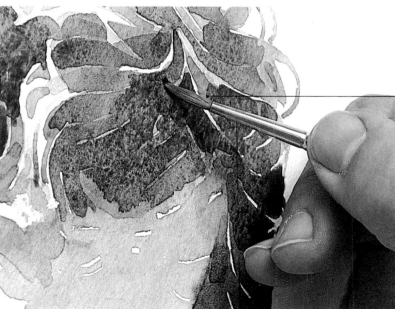

7. FINISHING THE HAIR
Wait until the hair area is completely dry, then work into this with a darker mixture of black and sepia, carefully painting in the shapes of the shadows. By strengthening these shadow areas – the spaces between the strands of hair – the hair itself is brought into sharper focus.

8. FACIAL FEATURES
Start to add the darker facial features, and develop the deeper shadow tones with brown madder, black and ultramarine. The gum water in the first wash will affect the colors, causing them to run, and then merge into softly defined edges.

9. FINISHING THE CLOTHING
Work into the overalls with a mixture of ultramarine and black, using a No.2 brush and picking out the main shadow areas. Paint the buttons with diluted raw umber.

10. FINAL TOUCHES
Add a few loosely painted
shadows to the girl's face,
defining and darkening the
tones. Finally, paint the lips
with a mixture of alizarin
crimson and raw umber.

BLUE IRISES

THIS PAINTING IS a study in simplification: the artist has depicted the vase of flowers by picking out certain elements, instead of attempting to imitate every detail of the subject. This is a highly recommended process, both for those who want to paint purely as an exercise, and for those wishing to create a finished picture which concentrates on definite points. In this case, the points emphasized are the fresh, simple colors, and their interplay with light. The painting progresses in simple stages from light to dark. Other elements and detail have been ignored, but one aspect has been deliberately exaggerated – the elongated shadow of the flowers which plays a crucial role in the composition.

The leaves are reduced to three tones – light, medium and dark – as are the petals of the flowers. The simplification continues with the glass jar, where flat white areas have been allowed to show through to depict reflections. The artist has paid close attention to the subject, noting that the lines of the stems are broken visually by the distorting effect water has on light and color. He has, therefore, carefully distorted the stems of the irises, as they enter the water.

A flat brown wash was all that was necessary to establish the tabletop. The background too is simplified to a thin wash, followed by a second layer of slightly darker, broken color. Without this top layer of textured paint, the background would have been flat.

WATERCOLOR PALETTE	
Sap Green	Lemon Yellow
Yellow Ochre	Ultramarine Blue
Alizarin Crimson	Raw Umber
Payne's Gray	
SUPPORT	
Bockingford paper, stretched 508 × 356mm (20 ×14in)	

1. FIRST STAGE
The delicate and specific shapes of the irises call for an accurate and careful approach. Start, therefore, by making a fine pencil drawing of the subject to act as a guide for the color. Using a diluted wash of sap green, lemon yellow and yellow ochre, block in the entire foliage area with what will eventually be the lightest tone of the leaves. Allow this to dry.

2. MEDIUM FOLIAGE TONES
Look for the medium tones on the leaves – those areas which are neither deep shadow nor pale highlights – and block them in with a slightly darker mixture of the sap green, lemon yellow, and yellow ochre. Simplify these middle tones into areas of flat color, without attempting to describe subtle tonal variation, or form. Again, let the paint dry before moving on to the next stage.

3. DEEP FOLIAGE TONES
Complete the foliage by painting in the actual subject's deepest color. As before, use a darker version of the general leaf color and work in flat areas. The green shadows seen through the glass are slightly darker, so flood the paint into these areas to create a deeper tone.

4. FLOWERS
Treat the flowers in exactly the same way as the foliage, by separating and simplifying the various colors in to three basic tones. For the lightest tone, paint an overall wash of ultramarine blue mixed with alizarin crimson, and allow this to dry.

5. MEDIUM TONES
With a darker wash of the same color, pick out the medium tones of the flowers. Paint the tiny yellow centers in yellow ochre and lemon yellow.

7. TABLETOP
Use a wash of raw umber, yellow ochre and alizarin crimson. Fill in the patches of tabletop visible behind the glass jar.

6. DARK TONES
Mix the third, and darkest flower color from ultramarine and alizarin, and paint in the deepest flower tones, paying particular attention to the folds and fluted creases on the petals. Paint these in exactly the same way as the leaves, in delicate shapes of flat color.

8. SHADOW
With raw umber and Payne's gray, paint the shadow thrown by the jar and flowers. Simplify the direction and shape of the shadow to create a strong, graphic effect.

9. FINISHING TOUCHES
Finally, block in the background wall with diluted Payne's gray, applied with loose textural brushstrokes. Allow this paint to dry, then, using a deeper version of the same color, extend the shadow shape up the wall with bold, angular brushstrokes. The exaggerated shadows add space and depth, and bring the composition convincingly to life.

MASKING

THE TECHNIQUE OF masking involves covering specific areas of the picture, so that they
will be protected while the paint is being applied. When the mask is removed, the areas
underneath will be untouched. This creative
method of making shapes is popular with many
artists and illustrators – not only can it be used
to produce clear, graphic shapes that give a
sense of design to a picture; it can also be
employed to facilitate working from light to
dark (*see pp 136-7*).

Certain methods of masking, such as using
the edges of pieces of paper, stencilling, or
employing masking tape, are better suited to
gouache than to pure watercolor; for unless you
use paint with a fairly thick consistency, the
colors will seep under the masks. These
methods are, in fact, more usually associated
with oil and acrylic, but gouache, although
water based, is often applied more thickly than
classic watercolor.

Masking fluid is ideal, however, for both
watercolor and gouache. It is a liquid, rubbery
solution which can be used to paint out specific
areas. When the fluid is dry, you can paint over
it, and the rubbery mask will protect the paper
underneath. Masking fluid is particularly useful
for working in watercolor from light to dark; for
instead of having to paint around each tiny, or
delicate shape that you wish to highlight in
white paper, or light tone, you can cover it
with masking fluid. You can practice this technique in the next project "On the Verandah"
(*see pp 152-5*), where tiny highlights will be
needed to create the texture of the chairs.

MASKING WITH COTTON
1. Place the blobs of cotton
on those areas which are to
be protected from the paint.
Spatter color over the surface
of the support, (including the
cotton) by dipping a small
decorator's brush in paint and
running your thumb over the
end of the bristles.
2. Lift up, and remove the
cotton, being careful to avoid
smudging the edges of the
covered areas.

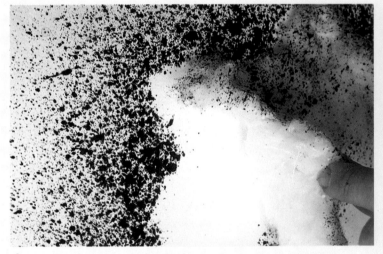

3. The result will be a clear, cut-
out area of white.

MASKING WITH TORN PAPER

1. This can only be done with fairly thick paint, so is best suited to gouache. Hold the torn paper mask in place, and apply the color firmly over the edge of the mask.

2. Lift the paper, being careful not to smudge the paint.

3. A torn paper mask produces a characteristic rugged edge, which would be very difficult to achieve with a brush.

MASKING FLUID

1. Paint the masking fluid over the areas which are to be left white. When the fluid is dry, paint over it with watercolor, or gouache. Let the paint dry.

2. Carefully remove the masking fluid by rubbing it with a clean finger, or an eraser.

MASKING TAPE

1. This technique is best suited to thick gouache. Press the tape firmly into position, and then take the color over its edge.

2. Wait for the paint to dry, and then carefully remove the tape.

3. The rubbed-away fluid will reveal graphically sharp shapes of white.

ON THE VERANDAH

MASKING FLUID has helped to transform this seemingly unlikely subject – two chairs on a verandah, in front of a pot of geraniums – into an arresting and unusual image. The fluid has enabled the artist to achieve a graphic painting, with sharply defined shapes and dramatic tonal contrasts. He painted the fluid onto the support before applying any paint, so that when the fluid was rubbed off, it would leave the tiny cutout shapes which so effectively represent the highlights on the woven chair seats.

With a simple subject like this, it is important to exploit to the full its inherent qualities – in this case the stark silhouettes, the texture of the chairs, and the sharply-defined negative shapes (the shapes of the spaces) contained within the chairs themselves. Therefore, instead of forcing the subject into a conventional composition, the artist opted for a symmetrical picture, by dividing the paper into equal halves: the composition is divided horizontally by the edge of the verandah, and vertically by the upright wooden post.

WATERCOLOR PALETTE	
Cobalt Blue	Alizarin Crimson
Payne's Gray	Sap Green
Sepia	Ivory Black
Cadmium Red	Brown Madder Alizarin
SUPPORT	
Stretched cartridge paper 356 × 457mm (14 × 18in)	

I. FIRST STAGE
Start by making a light line drawing of the subject. For this painting, the artist used an HB pencil, but you can use a softer one, providing the final lines are light enough not to show through the watercolor. Now, taking an old brush, paint masking fluid over those areas of the chairs which are to be left white.

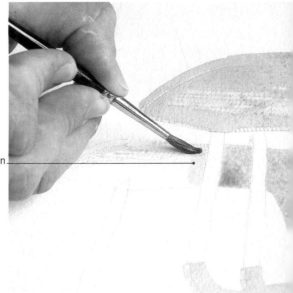

2. CHAIRS
When the masking fluid is dry, paint the chairs in a pale mixture of alizarin crimson, taking the color over the masking fluid.

3. SKY AND HILLS
Use a large wash brush to block in the sky with a very diluted wash of cobalt blue, and the distant hills with a mixture of Payne's gray, sap green and cobalt blue. Change to a No. 2 sable brush to paint around the shape of the pot of flowers.

4. DEVELOPING THE DETAILS
Still working over the dried masking fluid, paint a deeper, middle tone into the chairs with a mixture of alizarin and sepia. Paint the legs and arms of the chairs in Payne's gray, as well as the wooden post.

5. GERANIUM FOLIAGE
To paint the geranium leaves, simplify them into two tones of green. Start by establishing the entire foliage area with a very pale wash of sap green and Payne's gray. When this is dry, add more paint to the mixture and work the darker leaves in a stronger version of the same color.

6. COMPLETING THE GERANIUMS
Use two tones of Payne's gray for the plant pot, starting with an overall pale wash and, when this is dry, picking out the geranium shadows in a darker tone. Finally, mix cadmium red and brown madder alizarin, then delicately add flowers with a No. 2 sable brush.

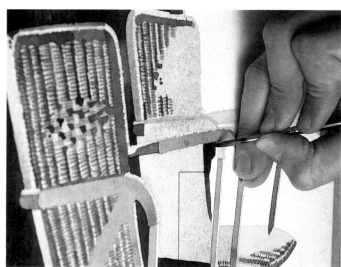

8. DEEPER CHAIR TONES
Mix alizarin crimson and Payne's gray, apply as shown, and leave to dry.

9. REMOVING MASKING FLUID
When the paint is completely dry, remove the masking fluid by rubbing it off with an eraser, or your finger.

7. THE VERANDAH
Paint the background in ivory black and sepia, using a No. 7 sable brush for the large expanses, and a No. 2 for taking the paint up to the outline of the chairs. Leave a strip of paper uncovered between the hills and the verandah color, as this will create the visual effect of a wall. Paint in a second darker wash on the wall, leaving the floor area in the lighter wash.

10. FINAL TOUCHES
Complete the painting by adding tiny shadows of alizarin crimson and Payne's gray to the wicker texture of the chair.

MONOCHROME

MONOCHROME MEANS restricting your palette to one color; with watercolor, however, this means you have the benefit of the white paper to lighten the tones.

Working in monochrome is an excellent exercise, because it makes you look for the tones in your subject. It is important that you should do this even when working in full color, so it is helpful to get into the habit of viewing an object in terms of its contrasting lights and darks. You need to find an interesting tonal composition – a balance of lights and darks – as well as being aware of its colors.

The choice of color for a monochrome picture is naturally important if it is to be the only one, since the whole range of tones, from light to dark, must derive from it. If you begin with a light color like yellow, your tonal range is severely limited to the light end of the tonal scale, from pale gray to white. Traditionally, black, sepia and brown are the colors chosen.

Look at your subject, as the artist has done here, and find the tonal equivalent of the color you see. For instance, any black in the subject will be the equivalent of the darkest tone of your chosen color, and white will be the white of the paper.

OBJECTS IN A WINDOW
The artist has picked out the tones of this subject, working in various strengths of Payne's gray. The darkest area, on the shaded sides of the duck and apples, are depicted in full strength color. The lightest tones are depicted by the white paper. On the right, you can see the results of working in red and green respectively.

A MISTY SCENE

WITH WATERCOLOR, it is possible to work literally in monochrome, without introducing white paint to lighten the tone of the selected color. In this way, by planning carefully, and by using the white of the paper, you can capture your subject in all its tones with just one color on the palette.

For this picture, the artist chose Payne's gray, a color which is so dark when undiluted that it is often used instead of black. By diluting it to varying degrees, he was able to explore an extremely broad range of tones, from the white of the paper to the very darkest gray of the paint.

The artist has made use of aerial perspective (*see pp 134-5*) to help establish a sense of space. He washed in the background with a very diluted tone, and then strengthened the shapes as they come nearer to the foreground.

A special technique was employed to create a misty atmosphere. The artist mixed gumwater with the initial wash; the gum suspended the pigment in the paint, which meant that much of the color was prevented from sinking into the paper. He then applied a damp sponge to the shapes of the distant trees: the gum dissolved, making the color easier to remove, and the resulting blurring gives the distant shapes their hazy quality.

The same technique was used on the foreground trees. Even though these were darker and more definite, they needed to be slightly blurred to convey a convincing sense of mist.

The composition relies on a simple juxtaposition of the foreground trees, with their strong shadows. The color was applied quite freely to these trees, giving a textural effect which rescued the picture from appearing too uniform.

WATERCOLOR PALETTE
Payne's Gray
SUPPORT
Bockingford paper, stretched 432 × 559mm (17 × 22in)

1. FIRST WASH
Restrict your palette to Payne's gray (light grays and whites are obtained by using the white tone of the paper). Start by blocking in the distant trees and fields with a diluted wash of Payne's gray mixed with a little gum arabic.

2. DARKER TONES
When the first tone is completely dry, paint in the nearer objects – the two trees and the hillock – with a darker wash of Payne's gray mixed with a little gum arabic. Allow this to dry.

3. SHADOWS
Paint in the tree shadows, and strengthen the trees themselves with a darker version of the same solution.

4. MIST
Soften the edges of the trees with a sponge, to create the impression of a scene being viewed through mist. The gum arabic mixed with the paint allows the color to be wiped off the paper easily without leaving a strong stain.

5. TEXTURE
Finally, strengthen the trees and shadows with darker color. Use the brushstrokes to represent the general texture of the foliage and the grass.

CREATING WHITE

WHITE PAPER IS A key element in watercolor painting, but you are not restricted simply to leaving areas of the support unpainted. There are other ways of exploiting the whiteness, some of which also add a textural dimension to the painting.

You can scratch the dried paint on the surface of the picture with matt knives, or any other sharp object, to reveal etched streaks, or specks of white. This technique, known as *sgraffito*, is particularly useful for texturing, lifting dull areas of color, creating the shimmering highlights on expanses of water, and making tiny, specific, highlighted areas. Sandpaper produces a similar, though more overall effect.

Color can sometimes be lifted by removing some of the paint while it is still wet. Any absorbent material, such as blotting paper, tissue, cotton, or Q-tips can be used for this, as well as for mopping up mistakes and unwanted areas of color. Domestic bleach, or gumwater, is also useful for lifting pigment to create pale areas.

In addition, some of the textural techniques mentioned on pages 172-5, such as wax resist, can be used for creating white, as can the masking technique described on pages 150-1.

SGRAFFITO

1. If the flat edge of a craft knife is scraped across the top relief of textured paper, it leaves a mottled, even effect.

2. Sandpaper has the same result, but gives a definite directional appearance to the etched white area.

3. Use the pointed end of a craft knife, or matt knife to etch hatched white lines in the color.

4. The sandpapered whiteness (bottom) produces a more evenly textured effect than the sharply etched matt knife lines (top).

BLEACH

1. Use an old paint brush to apply domestic bleach to the areas you wish to lighten.

2. Leave the bleach in place: the color will gradually lighten. With some pigments, it can also change the color slightly, so experiment first.

FINE LINES

1. To create finer lines with a sharp implement, first mix the color with gum arabic, and then scratch the surface before the paint is dry.

LIFTING COLOR

1. Large areas of wet color can be lifted by using blotting paper to soak up the wet color.

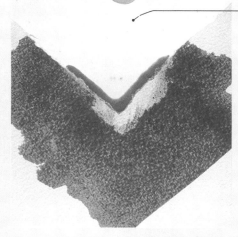

2. Quite small areas of wet color can be lifted with Q-tips.

2. The result will be a light feathery texture.

GUMWATER AND GUM ARABIC
1. Mixing a little gum arabic, or gumwater, with paint makes it easier to lift the color.

2. Apply the color to the paper, and allow it to dry.

3. Wet the areas which you want to lighten, with clean water.

4. Blot off the water. This will remove color, and reveal lightened areas.

STILL LIFE

IN THIS PAINTING, white has been created by scratching the paint surface, as well as by leaving areas of the white paper unpainted. The subject is ideally suited to this sgrafitto technique, because a considerable amount of wood is involved.

The artist used a matt knife to scratch prominent downward strokes on the pepper pot and wooden spoon, producing a typical pattern that also helped to create something of the warm atmosphere of a comfortable kitchen, with its familiar utensils. In the finished picture, the jug of utensils is placed upon a coarse wooden tabletop. Scratch marks have been scored with a knife, revealing specks of white – the light streaks of the grained wood. The artist also rubbed sandpaper firmly across the surface to lift the color and roughen the texture.

Notice, too, how the artist has adapted the setting of this still life. The original arrangement was on a white tabletop against a wood-chip background, but the artist decided to reverse the colors in the painting, so setting the utensils against a plain white background. The arrangement of a still-life subject can often be adjusted in such a way – many artists depart from the subject altogether, using it merely as a starting-off point.

The choice of objects in this arrangement was deliberate, however, as the artist wanted a variety of shapes and finishes.

WATERCOLOR PALETTE	
Brown Madder Alizarin	Yellow Ochre
Burnt Umber	Sepia
Sap Green	Ivory Black
Raw Umber	Cadmium Red
Payne's Gray	
SUPPORT	
Stretched Waterford paper (rough) 432 × 559mm (17 × 22in)	

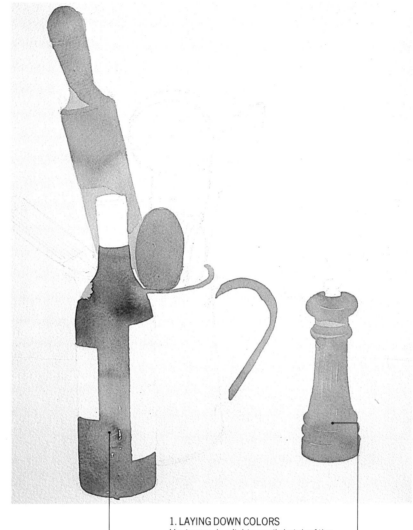

1. LAYING DOWN COLORS
Having made a light pencil sketch of the subject, start to paint the main areas of color. For the wooden objects, mix yellow ochre, brown madder alizarin, and burnt umber; by altering the ratios of the three slightly, you create the subtle color differences that distinguish the various woods. Use sap green with ivory black for the bottle.

2. BUILDING UP
Continue blocking in the local color of the objects with thin layers of color. Use cadmium red with brown madder alizarin for the ladle and bottle top; Payne's gray with a touch of yellow ochre for the metal utensils; and yellow ochre with a little Payne's gray for the jug. Working wet on dry, paint the shadows on the wooden spoon, pepper pot and rolling pin in a deeper version of the first color.

3. STRENGTHENING FORM
Develop the forms within the subject by darkening and defining the shapes of the shadows. For example, paint shadows on the ladle, spoon and bottle, taking care to make the shapes accurate, so as to describe the curved surfaces.

4. THE BOTTLE TOP
Here, the artist is painting the shadow on the bottle top with a darker mixture of cadmium red and sepia. Again, the shape of this shadow is used to describe the cylindrical form of the bottle neck.

5. THE TABLE
Paint the tabletop with a diluted mixture of raw umber, yellow ochre and Payne's gray. When this is dry, establish the shadows – Payne's gray and raw umber across the table, and Payne's gray with yellow ochre up the wall.

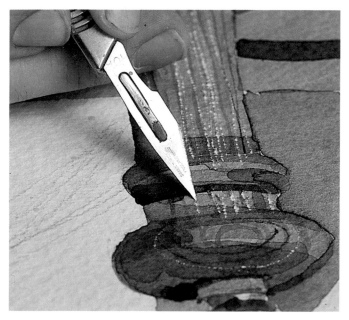

6. INTRODUCING TEXTURE
Having allowed the paint to dry thoroughly, start to introduce some texture into the areas of flat color. Here the artist is using the point of a matt knife to etch fine white lines on the pepper pot.

7. IMITATION GRAIN
By combining scratched white lines with the dark painted ones, the artist has created a convincing and effective imitation of wood grain. Notice how the pattern carefully follows the contours and curved form of the pepper pot. Similar textural marks and scratches are used elsewhere in the composition, such as on the rolling pin and tabletop.

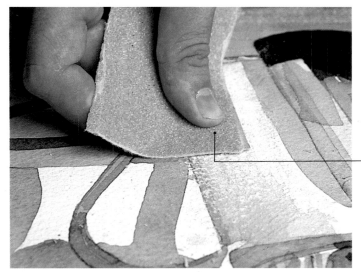

8. SANDPAPER TEXTURING
Use coarse sandpaper when a smooth, mottled texture is required. On rough watercolor paper, the sandpaper lifts the color from the raised parts of the surface to create a light, speckled effect.

9. THE FINISHED PICTURE
The finished picture shows how the artist has exploited several texture-making techniques, combining scratched marks, also known as "sgraffito", with loose pencil scribbling to break up the flat areas of color and so enliven the image. It also shows how the original still-life model has been adapted to suit the medium of watercolor.

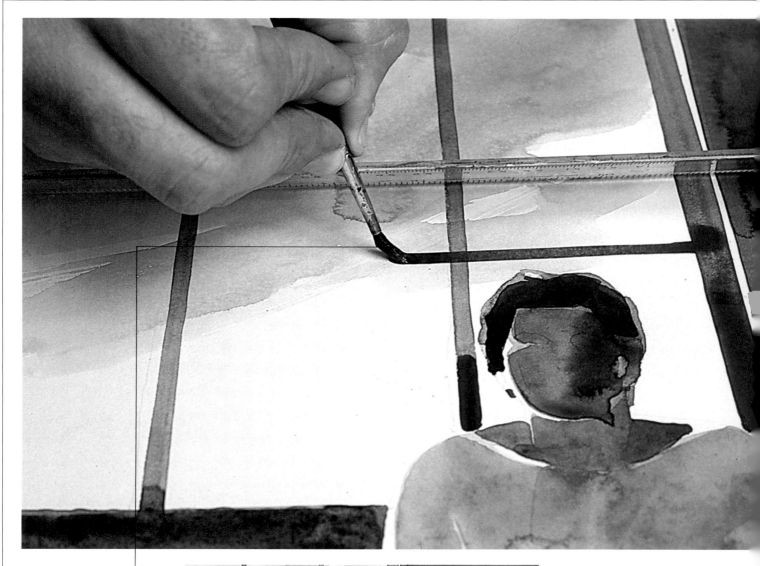

6. PAINTING THE WINDOW
When the sky is dry, use a ruler as a guide to help you paint the straight edges of the window frame. Mix some Payne's gray to a fairly thin consistency then, holding the edge of the ruler slightly above the paper, run your painting hand along it. Do not let the paint come into direct contact with the ruler, or allow the ruler to touch the paper, as otherwise the color will bleed and smudge.

7. FINISHING THE FRAME
Finish painting the window frame, using the ruler as a guide throughout. The starkness and graphic simplicity of the mechanically straight lines will help to create emphases and contrasts with the softer, irregular forms of the figure.

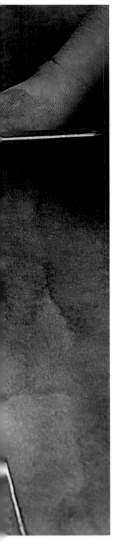

13

8. THE FOLIAGE
When the window frame is completely dry, paint the foliage with loose strokes of olive green and sap green.

9. THE FINISHED PICTURE
You can see just how important a role the white highlights play in the finished painting. They clearly separate the various elements, and divide what would otherwise be amorphous blobs of color into clearly defined forms. They also help to describe the forms themselves. Being the lightest planes in the picture, they represent the daylight as it falls upon the figure and seat.

CREATING TEXTURE

EVERYTHING IN REAL life has a texture, whether it is the choppiness of the sea, or the roughness of concrete. These surface characteristics can often be conveyed by brushwork; alternatively, you can sometimes texture the surface of the picture.

Texturing can be employed not only to represent the real-life appearance of the subject, but to enliven the actual paint surface of the picture itself. There are three basic methods of texturing surfaces: a brush can be used to apply broken color, spatters, speckles or other paint effects; paint can be applied by other means, such as a sponge; the paint can be made to react by applying substances such as wax to the paper, or by mixing the paint with an additive, such as gum arabic.

When gum arabic is mixed with paint, it gives the color a gloss and texture which retains the shape of the brushmarks when the paint is applied to the paper. The mixture can also be combed, or scratched with a texturing tool, to make a surface pattern. Paint mixed with gum arabic, or the thinner gumwater, can be dissolved easily when dry, because the gum suspends the pigment, prevents it from soaking into the paper, and prepares the way for some of the special effects illustrated.

It is important, however, to realize that texturing techniques can be overdone: a painting may be ruined by arbitrary marks. It is better to be selective, and only to apply a little texture to a particular area.

USING SALT
1. Sprinkling sea salt over wet paint is one way of creating a granular, textured effect.

2. Leave the salt for a few minutes, to allow it to absorb the wet color. When the paint is dry, brush away the grains of salt to reveal a mottled pattern.

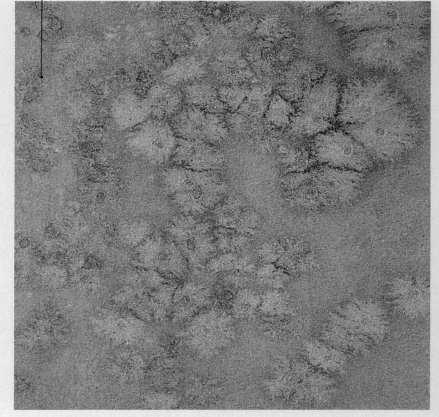

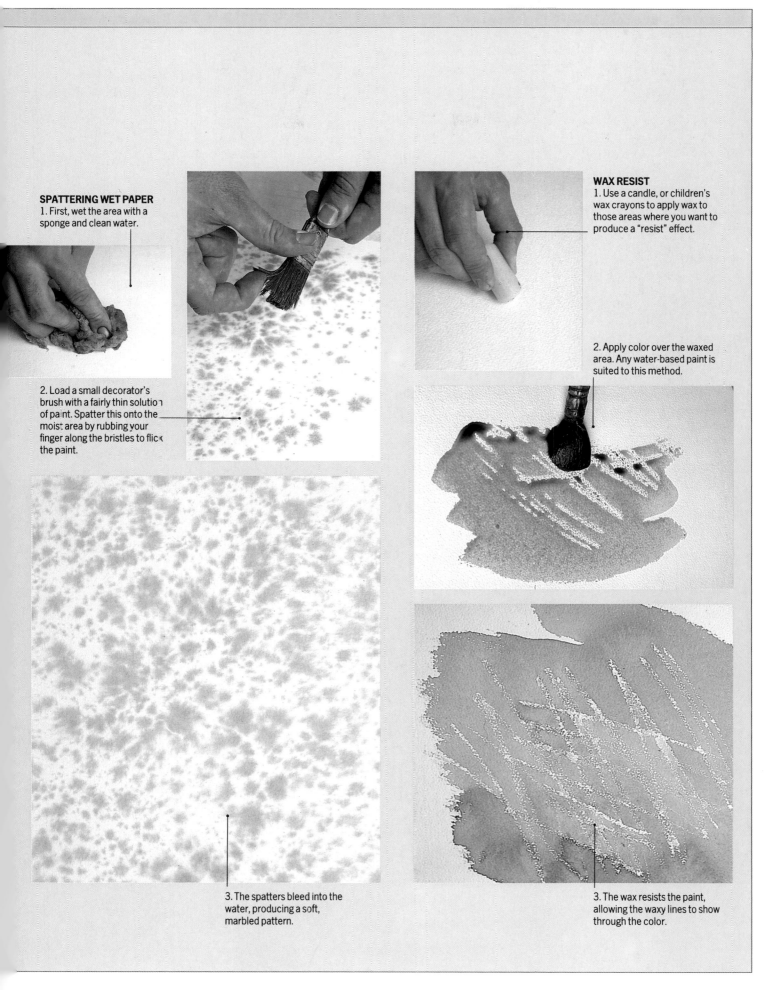

SPATTERING WET PAPER
1. First, wet the area with a sponge and clean water.

2. Load a small decorator's brush with a fairly thin solution of paint. Spatter this onto the moist area by rubbing your finger along the bristles to flick the paint.

3. The spatters bleed into the water, producing a soft, marbled pattern.

WAX RESIST
1. Use a candle, or children's wax crayons to apply wax to those areas where you want to produce a "resist" effect.

2. Apply color over the waxed area. Any water-based paint is suited to this method.

3. The wax resists the paint, allowing the waxy lines to show through the color.

USING A SPONGE

1. Mix a solution of paint, dip a natural sponge into it, and dab color onto the paper.

2. This technique produces a broken texture, with a smooth quality.

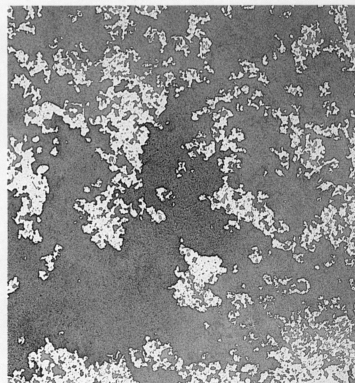

3. Follow the above procedure, but use a synthetic sponge.

4. The result, in this case, is a more spiky, speckled effect.

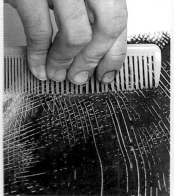

GUM ARABIC

1. Mix gum arabic with your color to thicken the paint, and give it a resinous quality. Apply the mixture to the paper. Because of its thickness and stickiness, you can create a texture in a variety of ways, including the combing effect shown.

2. The thickened paint retains the marks made by the comb.

3. Alternatively, you can use a brush to produce finer marks. Here, the artist is using a nailbrush.

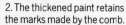

4. The result is a fine, hair-like texture.

SPATTERING WITH GUM ARABIC

1. Cover the surface with paint which has been mixed with gum arabic. Allow the paint to dry. Using a decorator's brush, spatter the paint with flecks of water.

2. Blot the dampened paint with clean tissue, or a rag.

3. The water lifts the color, forming a granular pattern

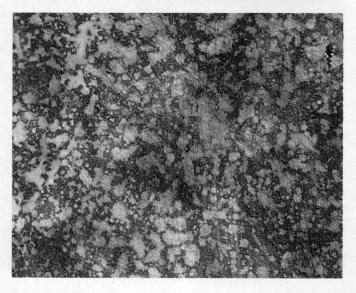

7. TEXTURING THE SHELL
To depict the coarse, pitted texture of the crab: spatter a little of the lightest tone across the shell by dipping a small decorator's brush in a fairly thin mixture of color and then, holding the brush a short distance from the paper, run your fingers along its bristles. Finally, rework some of the dark tones on the shell and legs.

8. THE PLATE
Add the decorative ring around the plate in ultramarine blue, darkened with a little black. Mix this color with white, and use a large wash brush to paint the curved shadow which describes the rounded form of the plate.

14

9. UNDER-SHADOW
Mix raw umber, black and a little cadmium orange; then paint the shadow under the plate, using the large brush to achieve a continuous, curved shape.

10. WOOD GRAIN
Use this same shadow color to indicate the wood grain in the tabletop with thin horizontal lines. When the paint is dry, firmly drag a sheet of coarse sandpaper horizontally across the table area to emphasize the granular texture of the wood.

11. FINISHED PICTURE
The completed painting reveals how the artist has used a limited range of colors, building up the forms in tonal planes with opaque gouache paint. The dull, matt surface of the gouache is enlivened by the texture: spattered color on the crab, and the sandpapered grain of the wooden table.

7. THE RESIST
Using an ordinary domestic candle, rub wax across the dry, gray paint of the chapel wall. This creates the necessary resist for the next watercolor wash.

8. CREATING THE STUCCO
Apply more of the ivory black and yellow ochre mixture to the building, this time painting over the waxed areas. The raised texture of the rough paper holds the candlewax and so resists the paint; color seeps into the crevices, helping to create the effect of stuccoed walls.

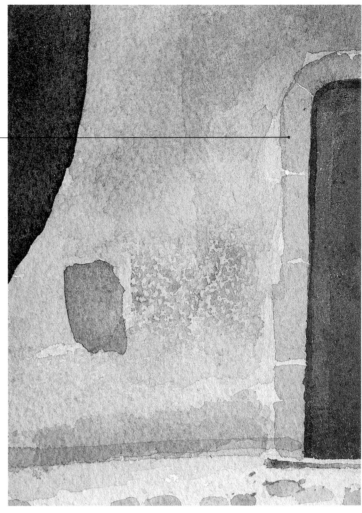

9. COBBLES AND TREE
Develop the foreground, suggesting the cobblestones with various mixtures of Payne's gray, yellow ochre and sepia. Then mix Hooker's green, sap green and Payne's gray with a little gum water and use this to strengthen the color of the cypress tree. Allow to dry.

10. TREE TEXTURE
Sprinkle a little water onto the tree, and immediately dab this off with a clean, dry tissue or cloth. The gum water allows the top layer of paint to come off easily with the water, leaving a leafy, mottled texture on the tree.

15

11. THE FINISHED PICTURE
In the finished picture, the subtle textures on the tree and building help to bring the scene alive, introducing a rugged, almost tactile quality to the painting.

SNOW SCENE

THIS IS A VERY simple, but effective, scene, created with a minimum of brushstrokes. The strokes themselves play an important part in depicting the crisply marked surface of the snow, and the stark green trees. The artist painted the latter by loading a small brush with color and rolling it over the surface to create the jagged impression of conifer branches. Similarly, the marks and shadows in the snow are also described by brushstrokes – large, loose strokes for the shadows, and small calligraphic marks to indicate the frozen grass poking up through the snow.

Another important piece of texturing in the picture is the white spattering to indicate falling snow. This is not done evenly, for this would have given the painting an unconvincing "Christmas card" look. Instead, the spattering was irregularly and lightly scattered across the image, which works particularly effectively on the dark, almost silhouetted shapes of the trees.

WATERCOLOR PALETTE	
Payne's Gray	Indigo
Sepia	Sap Green
Gouache	
Titanium White	
SUPPORT	
Bockingford paper, stretched 406 × 559mm (16 × 22in)	

1. THE FIRST WASH
Splash a wash of Payne's gray and indigo loosely across the sky and shadow areas of the ground. Do this quickly with a wash brush.

2. SHADOW AND DETAIL
When the first wash is dry, strengthen some of the shadows with a darker version of the same color. Change to a smaller brush, such as a No. 2 sable, and use it with a mixture of sepia and Payne's gray to suggest animal tracks and dead grass in the snow. Try not to work tightly and to retain the dry, feathery nature of the subject, representing the snow by rolling the brush loosely across the paper.

3. THE TREES
Mix sepia, Payne's gray and sap green for the trees. Still working with the smaller brush, roll the color onto the picture, creating dark broken streaks to represent the spiky branches of the firs.

4. PAINTING SHADOWS
Take a little of the tree color and paint the shadows, blending these into the surrounding areas with clean water.

5. THE FOREGROUND
Strengthen the foreground with sepia, mixed with a little Payne's gray. The warm sepia provides an effective contrast to the cold grays and greens elsewhere in the composition. Apply the color in short, quick strokes.

6. SPATTERING SNOWFLAKES
Mix white gouache to a fairly runny consistency and, with a small decorator's brush, spatter this across the scene to represent snowflakes.

7. MAXIMIZING EFFECT
Take care not to overdo your spattering. A few spatters on some of the darker areas, such as the trees, is more effective and convincing than a film of regular white dots over the whole picture. Stop working on the picture as soon as you have finished applying the snow.

8. THE FINISHED PICTURE
The freshness and crispness of the final image comes from working rapidly and knowing when to stop. The aim is to create an impression, rather than emphasizing specific details; you should rely on the brushstrokes themselves to describe the subject.

DRYBRUSH

A VERY DISTINCTIVE, subtle texture can be achieved by using what is known as "drybrush" technique. Squeeze, or wipe the moisture from the brush until the bristles are almost dry. When the paint is applied to the paper, the result has a feathery quality. This characteristic can be increased, and controlled, if you press your thumb against the top of the bristles to splay them in a fan shape.

The American painter, Andrew Wyeth is one of the leading exponents of drybrush technique (*see p. 64*). He uses it tonally – first applying a light wash, and then covering it with a slightly darker tone of the same color, painted with a drybrush. Wyeth often employs this technique to convey the directional texture of grass, or the coarse surfaces of walls and buildings.

DRYBRUSH MARKS

1. With the brush squeezed almost dry, use short, directional strokes to create a loose, feathery texture.

2. For a vertical pattern, make upward and downward strokes in a loose, sweeping manner.

3. First, apply loose blobs of dark gray color, and then drybrush a lighter tone over these, to create a loose, textured effect.

4. Dip the dried brush in paint, splay the bristles into a fan shape, and then drag the color across the paper in regular horizontal strokes.

STILL LIFE WITH DRYBRUSH

This still life of a jug of flowers relies on the drybrush technique to bring the picture to life. There is a large amount of space around the subject; therefore, texturing the background and the tabletop has added interest to the composition.

1. The background has been textured by drybrushing Payne's gray onto a lighter tone. This breaks up the flatness of the large expanse of wall behind the flowers.

2. When painting the tabletop, the artist reversed the color scheme, drybrushing an opaque light tone over a dark gray undercolor.

WINDOWS AND SHUTTERS

THERE IS LITERALLY no space in this unusual picture; foreground, middle and far distance are all equally absent. Everything is flat – in complete opposition to the normal type of composition, which presents the viewer with an illusion of depth. The task of the artist was to find ways of counteracting the flatness, which could easily make this picture very dull.

The method chosen by the artist was to create the illusion of texture and shadows, though in achieving the former, care had to be taken not to overdo the effect, as a flamboyant surface would have looked unrealistic. The answer was to use drybrush to represent the gritty, gravelly nature of the plaster finish on the wall. First a light wash was applied, and then subsequent tones and shadows were built up with drybrush, so allowing the first wash to show through in broken areas.

The area of brickwork was small, but it had a textural quality that needed to be brought out as well. The bricks were painted separately, using different proportions of the same color mix, some light and some dark.

Apart from this, the painting is extremely simple, with dark window panes, black graphic lines around them, and plain gray shutters. Though simple to create, the shadows of the shutters are important, as they help to offset the flatness of the composition.

Looking at the finished picture demonstrates just how the drybrush technique, plus some careful painting of brickwork and shadow, has brought this strange composition to life. It shows how, if not overdone, textures can make a painting interesting. Here, the sunlight beats down upon an empty wall, while a deep, cool, rather mysterious darkness seems to dwell inside the windows.

WATERCOLOR PALETTE	
Sepia	Payne's Gray
Ivory Black	Indigo
Ultramarine	Hooker's Green
SUPPORT	
Waterford paper, stretched 508 × 356mm (20 × 14in)	

1. STARTING OFF
Start by lightly sketching in the position of the windows, roof and hedge. Then apply a thin wash of sepia to the roof and a mixture of Payne's gray and indigo to the house wall.

2. BREAKING UP FLATNESS
Apply a lighter tone of Payne's gray and indigo to the front of the house with a wash brush. Allow this to dry, then work over the area again, using loose textural brushstrokes of the same color to break up the flatness of the initial wash.

3. PAINTING THE BRICKS
Use a flat-bristled brush to paint in the bricks, using regular, single brushstrokes and allowing these to dictate the shape of each brick. Use sepia and Payne's gray, changing the proportions of the mix as necessary to vary the tone of the bricks.

4. DRYBRUSH
Block in the window shutters with black and ultramarine. When these are dry, work over the flat wall again with a mixture of indigo and Payne's gray, using drybrush. To do this, squeeze the excess water from the bristles before dipping the brush in the paint, and then literally scrub color on to the wall. Use a darker shade of the same colors for the shadows under the window.

5. THE HEDGE
Paint the hedge in Hooker's green and black, mixed with gum water to give a sheen to the color.

6. FINE DETAIL
Use a fine brush, such as a No. 2 sable, to paint the narrow shadows around the windows, under the eaves, and on the shutters in indigo and black. Darken the hedge area with a deeper version of the same color.

7. FINISHING TOUCHES
Add the final details. Here the artist is using a ruler to aid the positioning of the dark lines of the window frames.

8. THE FINISHED PICTURE
The chosen subject, with its
deliberate flatness and lack of
scale or distance, relies for
interest on its inherent
textures. The most important
of these is the roughened wall
which the artist has used an
overall drybrush technique to
depict.

WARM AND COOL COLORS

THE COLOR WHEEL on page 94 reflects the fact that colors can be roughly divided into two main types – warm and cool. Blues, greens and purples are the cool colors, and reds, oranges and yellows are the warm ones. You will rarely see anything in real life which does not contain both warm and cool hues, although one type may predominate. This means that both warm and cool colors are likely to feature in nearly every picture you paint, and that it is important to strike a harmony between the two. Even the snow scene on page 184, which has a very chilly feel, is offset by a faintly warm shadow containing touches of sepia.

It is difficult to identify the color temperature of any hue in isolation, although the more extreme ones like bright red are obvious. For instance, yellow is generally regarded as a warm color; but if two yellows are placed next to each other, one an acid-lemon and the other a gold, then the lemon appears quite cold and the gold warm. Neutrals too have a color temperature. If you see a range of different grays together, it will immediately become apparent that some of them are bluish and some brownish and that, therefore, some are tending towards cool and others towards warm.

For the painter, depicting the counterplay of warm and cool colors on the human skin is probably one of the most important aspects of color temperature. The shadows are generally darker and cooler, containing grays, blues or greens; while the parts of the face, or figure on which normal light falls are predominantly composed of warm tones. This applies to all skin types. In the portrait on page 200, the artist has constructed the face from planes of cool dark and light warm washes of color.

STILL LIFE WITH COOL, OR WARM COLORS

The mood of a painting can be significantly changed, depending on the predominance of warm or cool colors. These two pictures are identical, except for the fact that the artist has shifted the emphasis of color temperature from cool (left) to warm (right).

195

APPLES ON A PLATE

THIS EXERCISE SHOWS you how to make the most of warm and cool colors. The apples, the focal point of the picture, are red and green – in other words, warm and cool – but the artist has exploited the inter-relationships between warm and cool colors elsewhere in his composition as well. The warm brown tones of the wooden tabletop, for instance, contrast with the cold gray of the background, together with the blue gray shadows of the plate and the area around the apples.

The apples are painted wet on wet, so that the red and green colors merge naturally, forming a brownish neutral join. Where the colors meet, they are not overworked. They are allowed simply to fuse slightly and dry; otherwise they could have become muddy and the colors would have lost their freshness as a result.

Symmetry and rigid divisions could have spoiled this composition had the artist not taken conscious steps to avoid them. The plate of apples was therefore slightly offset, and placed low on the paper. The edge of the table divides the picture diagonally; to avoid splitting the image into two separate halves, this edge is subtly interrupted by one of the apples, thus avoiding a stark division.

WATERCOLOR PALETTE	
Sap Green	Yellow Ochre
Alizarin Crimson	Raw Umber
Payne's Gray	
SUPPORT	
Stretched cartridge paper 356 × 508mm (14 × 20in)	

1. BLOCKING IN
Having made a light outline pencil drawing of the subject, block in the apples with a pale wash of sap green and yellow ochre, leaving white areas of paper for the highlights. While the paint is still wet, use Q-tips to soak up the color from those parts of the fruit which are to be painted red.

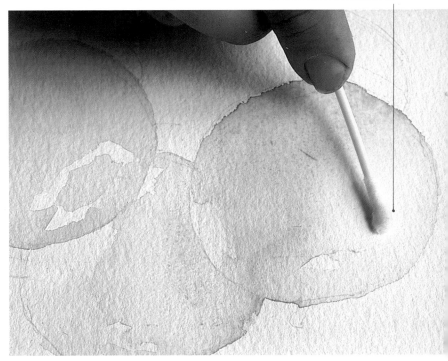

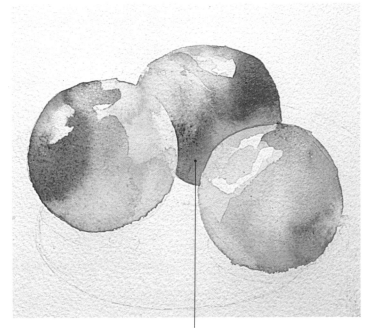

2. THE CHEEKS
Mix alizarin crimson with raw umber and apply this to the white areas on the apples to create the red cheeks. Work quickly, without allowing the paint to dry. If necessary, you can re-wet the area with clean water. The warm red bleeds into the damp green, the result being a natural looking contour and a gradual merging of the two colors.

3. APPLE SHADOWS
Paint a little raw umber into the apples while they are still wet, allowing this to merge into the red and green. This slightly darker tone represents the lighter shadows on the fruit; its use means that you are starting to describe the round form of the apples.

4. DEEPENING SHADES
For the deepest shading, mix Payne's gray with a little alizarin crimson and apply this to the darkest shadows on the fruit. Again, painting "wet on wet", allows the cool tone to merge naturally into the warm reddish brown on the apple.

5. THE PLATE
Mix a thin wash of Payne's gray
to depict the edge of the plate
and to suggest the shadows
that lie underneath the apples.

6. BLOCKING IN
Use a thin solution of raw umber to
block in the table, working with a wash
brush and darkening the wash slightly
towards the foreground of the picture.
Suggest the wood grain with darker
streaks of the same color.

7. THE PLATE AREA
Paint the shadow around the plate in Payne's gray, and then develop and strengthen the tones on the plate itself to match this.

8. THE BACKGROUND
Finally, paint the background in Payne's gray, making sure that the tone of this is of approximately the same strength as the darkest shadow areas on the main subject.

THE ARTIST'S FATHER

A CENTRAL FEATURE of this graphic portrait is the use of warm and cool colors in the flesh tones – an area of painting which has tested the skills of artists for centuries. Where human flesh is concerned, the highlights are usually warmer and lighter than they would otherwise be, while the shadows are cooler and darker. These principles have been adopted, refined and adapted by artists through the centuries, all of whom have developed their own individual touches. Here, too, the artist has followed a personal approach, using brown madder alizarin, cadmium orange and sepia for the warm areas, and Payne's gray, indigo and black for the cooler ones. These have been applied as thin overlapping layers of color, picking out the planes of light and shade on the model's face. The deepest shadows, around the eyes and eye sockets and underneath the chin and neck, are predominantly cool gray, with discernable touches of warmer tone relating them to the rest of the face. The strongest light tones, down the lefthand side of the face, are depicted by the color of the white paper.

The background is blocked in with sap green and gumwater, giving it a lively textural quality and enriching the color of the paint. This creates a pleasing contrast with the figure itself, which is actually quite flat – an effect caused mainly by the clothes. The shirt and jacket are painted as light, flat areas.

WATERCOLOR PALETTE

Brown Madder Alizarin	Cadmium Orange
Sepia	Payne's Gray
Indigo	Ivory Black
Sap Green	Cadmium Red
Raw Umber	

SUPPORT

Stretched cartridge paper
406 × 558mm (16 × 22in)

1. STARTING POINT
Start by blocking in the warm, light tones of the face with an extremely diluted wash of brown madder alizarin and cadmium orange. You may find it helpful to start with the forehead, and then to establish the position of the eye sockets with cooler shadows. Though it is not essential, you may also find it useful to make a light pencil drawing before you begin to paint. Then develop the shadow tones, working slowly and building up the layers of tone gradually. Generally, you should wait for each area to dry before proceeding, but occasionally lay some paint wet on wet, as this makes the skin tones blend slightly.

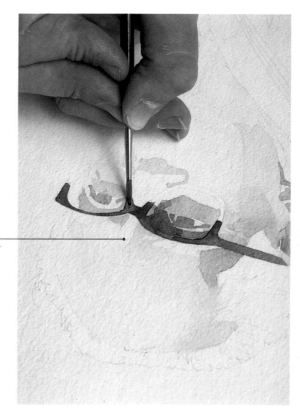

2. GLASSES FRAMES
Use the tip of the brush – the artist here is using a No. 4 sable – to paint the frames of the glasses with Payne's gray and raw umber. The solid color of the glasses provides a useful tone against which the strengths of subsequent lights and darks can be assessed.

3. FACE AND HAIR
Continue to build up the face tones. For the warm areas use brown madder alizarin and cadmium orange, occasionally adding sepia and a little Payne's gray to vary the color and tone of a particular area. For the cooler, dark shadows, mix indigo, black and more Payne's gray with the warmer color. Allow the whiteness of the paper to represent bright highlights. Paint the hair in indigo and black.

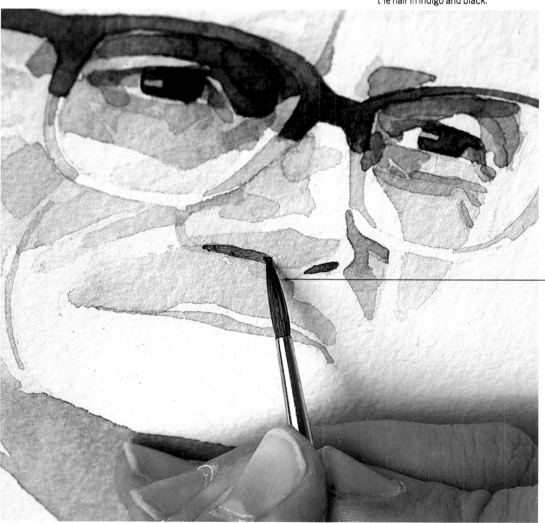

4. CREATING THE FORM
Work down the face, building up and overlapping tiny areas of warm and cool planes to create the form. Paint in the dark tones of the eyes and nostrils in Payne's gray mixed with a little of the flesh mix.

6. THE JACKET
Use Payne's gray for the jacket. Paint this as a flat shape, but allow more color to flood into shaded areas, such as the shadows under the collar and the wrinkles of the sleeves.

5. DEVELOPING SHADOWS
Develop the main shadows, blocking in the cool area under the chin in Payne's gray and indigo mixed with a little of the warmer skin tone. Look carefully at the shape of this shadow, which helps describe the form of the chin, throat and neck. When the neck area is completely dry, block in the shirt as a flat shape, using cadmium red toned with a little sepia. Allow this to dry.

7. THE BACKGROUND
Paint the background in sap green mixed with gum water, using a wash brush to create bold, broken texture. The gum water enriches the paint, so producing a slightly glossy surface. This creates a nice contrast with the thin, somewhat matt surface of the figure.

8. ADJUSTING TONES
The new rich background inevitably affects the tones on the figure, making some of them look faded and drab in comparison. Here, the artist is working into the shadows on the clothing, considerably darkening these to match the background tone.

9. FINISHING TOUCHES
In the finished picture, the tones have been substantially developed, both to emphasize the form of the figure and to strengthen the subject in relation to the surrounding background.

DARK TO LIGHT

WORKING FROM dark to light is only possible with opaque paint; gouache, therefore, is an ideal medium. This technique gives the artist more freedom than the traditional watercolor method of painting from light to dark (*see pp 136-7*). When painting with gouache, you do not have to decide in advance which areas will remain light; instead you can change the painting as you work, and add light touches at later stages, just as with oils. However, you must still work quickly, remembering that gouache is also a water-soluble paint: for instance, if you have painted a red flower, and you then add a yellow center to it, you will find that the underlying red will mix into the new wet paint, if you work it around too much.

Gouache is frequently combined with pure watercolor, particularly for adding paler details and highlights. This technique has been employed for centuries; the early watercolorists made use of what they called "body color", which was in fact a form of gouache.

CREATING FORM
Whereas the cylinder on pages 136-7 is built up from light to dark in transparent washes, the approach here is reversed. Using opaque paint, start with an overall dark color then gradually build up successive layers of light tone. Finally, add the lightest color to the top of the cylinder.

 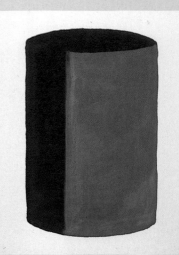

BUILDING UP TONE
When using gouache, light colors can be applied over dark ones. Unless the gouache is very diluted, the top pale color completely hides the color beneath.

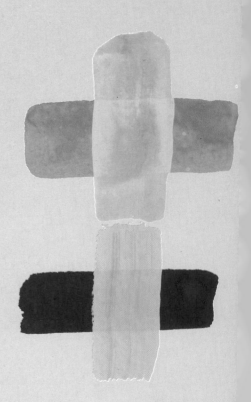

JARS WITH DRIED FLOWERS

THE OPAQUE QUALITY of gouache has been exploited to the full to create this fresh, colorful painting, which is full of earth tones highlighted by touches of reflected daylight. Starting from the warm tone of a piece of tinted card, the artist has used the opaque paint to work lighter tones onto darker ones.

Though the technique is slightly unconventional, there are still parallels with classical watercolor procedure. The gouache has been heavily diluted, producing a thinner mixture. Parts of the support have been allowed to show through as well – just as white paper does in traditional light-to-dark watercolor.

The tinted card plays a positive role, since its warm tone suits the subject's main elements, which are depicted in warm natural beiges and browns. The chairback, for instance, is left untouched, showing through the painting as a beige silhouette.

The flowers form a splash of color in the middle of the earthy tones. These are created in traditional gouache style, working from dark to light. The artist has blocked in the flower areas with deeper tones – usually the local color of the flower with black added to darken it. In this way, the main shapes of the heads of the flowers have been established. Then brighter, lighter colors are applied, brushstrokes being used to describe the different types of petals and flower characteristics – as with the short, spiky strokes used to paint the chrysanthemums.

WATERCOLOR PALETTE	
Gouache	
Jet Black	Yellow Ochre
Raw Umber	Burnt Sienna
Cadmium Yellow	Lemon Yellow
Titanium White	Ultramarine Blue
Cadmium Red	Alizarin Crimson
SUPPORT	
Sepia colored card 533 × 533mm (21 × 21in)	

1. INITIAL BLOCKING
Decide how you want to position the subject in the picture, and make a simple pencil drawing to establish this. Then, working from an initial palette of black, white, yellow ochre, raw umber and burnt sienna gouache, start to block in the darkest tones of the subject.

2. DEVELOPING THE TONES
Without allowing the dark tones, to dry, develop the subject by adding the lighter tones and some local color. Use black and raw umber for the teapot; raw umber, cadmium red and black for the rim of the center jar; and mix white with a little of the local color to paint in the lighter tones elsewhere.

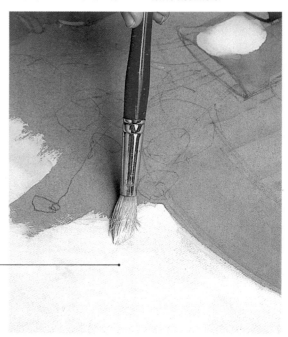

3. THE BACKGROUND
Block in the large background areas in white mixed with a little raw umber and yellow ochre, working with a large brush (here a No. 12 Dalon watercolor brush is being used).

4. WORKING UP
Change to a smaller brush – a No. 6 is ideal – and take the background tone up to the subject, making the strokes clean and confident, so that the chair and the objects on the table stand out as strong, graphic statements.

5. DESCRIBING THE TEAPOT
Now, turn your attention to the objects themselves. Work into these, applying broad planes of light and shade in order to describe their forms. The white jug, for example can be depicted in just two tones – both mixed from varying proportions of white, yellow ochre and black. Similarly, develop the teapot and the earthenware pot next to it, working in two or three tones of the appropriate colors. Because the objects are glossy, the highlights are almost white, modified with a small quantity of local color.

6. FLOWER HEADS
Start to paint the flower heads, positioning them carefully and correctly in relation to one another. Paint the darkest, dullest tone of each flower first as a flat shape – for example, for the red flowers, mix cadmium red with a little black and use cadmium yellow, white and black for the yellow ones.

7. HIGHLIGHTS AND COLOR
When you start to develop the flowers, use a No. 4 sable brush to add bright highlights and color to the petals. The opacity of the paint enables you to paint light tones over darker ones quite easily.

8. TEXTURE AND DETAIL
Look carefully at the texture and character of each bloom, choosing and manipulating your brushstrokes to depict the petals on each type of flower accurately.

9. FLOWER DETAIL
Use cadmium yellow, lemon yellow and white to dot in the bright flecks on the large yellow flower; ultramarine and white for the blue flower; cadmium red, cadmium yellow and white for the bright red flower; and alizarin and white for the bright pink bloom.

10. THE FINISHED PAINTING
The warm, harmonious tones of the finished painting are greatly enhanced by the choice of sepia colored stationer's – not artist's – card as the support. The earthy sepia is allowed to show through deliberately in places, reflecting the general color theme of the subject and helping to hold together the separate elements.

SUNLIT FIELD

THE OPAQUE QUALITY of gouache allowed the artist to work light onto dark to produce a vividly graphic picture of countryside flooded with sunlight. The graphic approach is a characteristic of this particular artist, who has worked as an illustrator, and the composition is seen very much in terms of shape, color and tone. It works as an abstract arrangement as well as a landscape. Linear elements, such as the barbed wire fence, have been introduced, together with a variety of textures which contrast with the slightly stylized way in which the artist has simplified the composition.

The artist wanted to tint the background – a classical painting technique. However, this popular method (usually employed by oil painters) in which the canvas is toned before starting, is impossible with ordinary watercolor because of its transparency; neither can the ground be tinted with gouache, because even when dry the paint is still soluble. For a specific tint you can lay down a coat of insoluble acrylic paint first. In this case, however, the artist found a sheet of medium-tone green paper which was perfectly suited to the color scheme. With this medium tone already established, lighter and darker tones, related to the tone of the paper, could then be added.

WATERCOLOR PALETTE

Gouache	
Sap Green	Sepia
Ivory Black	Yellow Ochre
Titanium White	Cadmium Yellow
Ceruleum	

SUPPORT

Green tinted paper
356 × 508mm (14 × 20in)

1. FIRST STAGE
Working on medium-toned green paper, start by making a light outline drawing. Then, using the color of the paper as a middle tone, look for the darkest tone present in the subject – in this case, the shadows in the tree foliage. Mix this color from sap green, sepia and ivory black, and paint in the shadow shapes with a No. 2 sable brush. Use the same color for the tree trunk.

2. GRASS
Loosely wash in the field, using a light wash of yellow ochre and sap green, and a wash brush. Leave patches of the paler paper showing through to represent the light areas of the grass.

3. FENCE
Paint the fence in a mixture of ivory black and sepia, with a No. 2 sable brush.

4. NEGATIVE SHAPES
Mix titanium white and cadmium yellow for the sunlit field, and pick out the negative shapes – the shapes of the spaces – between the fence posts. Take the light yellow carefully up to the dark posts, defining the shapes and throwing the fence into sharp, linear silhouette against its paler background.

5. SKY
For the sky, mix white with a little ceruleum blue. Use this to dot in the tiny fragments of sky showing between the leaves, and to block in the larger expanse behind the tree.

6. GRASS TEXTURE
Scribble in the grass texture with bold, jagged pencil strokes. Here, the artist uses a green pencil, and an ordinary graphite drawing pencil to suggest tall, wavy grass.

7. BARBED WIRE FENCE
Paint the fence posts closest to the foreground in white: start by blocking them in with a thin wash, developing the form with streaks of more opaque color. Draw in the barbed wire with a graphite stick.

8. BARBED WIRE
Draw the top strand of barbed wire with a fine, light gray pencil line.

9. FINISHING TOUCHES
By using light and dark tones on medium-toned paper, the artist has successfully and graphically captured the effect of sunlight and flickering shadows in this rural scene. The textures are subtle but varied, providing just enough contrast with the matt gouache paint to transform an arrangement of flat shapes into a lively and unusual pictorial composition.

WATERCOLOR PENCILS

USE WATERCOLOR PENCILS as you would ordinary colored pencils, to work in loose scribbles, or in quite fine, precise detail. When you have completed the picture, or a stage of the picture, with pencils, you can use a wet brush to blend the colors.

You will never have quite the same control over the result as you would with watercolor paint, because when you wet a colored pencil mark, the color often becomes darker and brighter. If your pencil strokes are too heavy in the first place, especially with the dark colors, then the water will be unable to dissolve the lines completely, and the pencil marks will show through. Practice is vital, so that you will know what to expect.

Watercolor pencils are probably most effective when water is used only on parts of the painting. This creates a contrast between the "painted", and the textural, pencilled areas.

Not all supports are suitable for this recent medium. Some watercolor papers, particularly the more textured ones, tend to disintegrate. When the artist tried to blend colors for the project, "Woman by a Window" (*see pp 216-9*), he found that the surface lifted off some papers. Finally, he chose a smooth illustration board.

WORKING ON WET
1. Moisten each area of the paper, just before you start working on it.

2. Scribble on the moist area with one color.

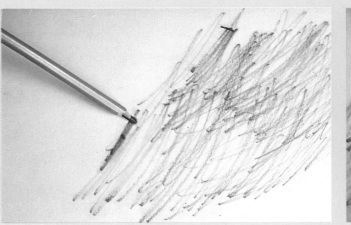

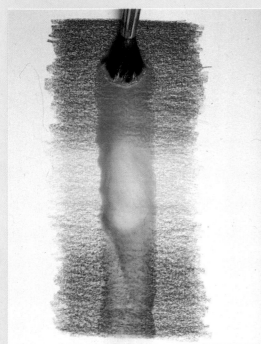

A wet brush drawn through a spectrum of watercolor pencil marks, shows how the colors react to water. Experiment freely to obtain particular effects.

4. The colors blend as they bleed into the wet paper.

TRADITIONAL METHOD

1. The traditional method of drawing with watercolor pencils is to treat them like ordinary pencils. One color can be drawn on top of another.

2. To mix the colors, dip a soft brush into clean water and blend them together smoothly.

3. Scribble a second color over the first, using loose strokes, and being careful not to make the color too dense.

3. The result is similar to pure watercolor paint.

WOMAN BY A WINDOW

IN THIS LOOSELY worked composition of a woman looking out at the view from her window, the artist has fully exploited the versatility of watercolor pencils. These are sometimes used as ordinary colored pencils, to create a scribbly broken texture in certain areas, and sometimes as traditional watercolor paints to create smoother patches of blended color. There is an interesting contrast, for instance, between the treatment of the interior – the figure and the room, both of which are rendered in bold textural pencil strokes – and the view through the window. The artist decided to make the exterior scene into a watercolor "painting" by dissolving the colors. Thus, a picture within a picture has been created, while looseness, too, is one of the central themes. Even the figure, the focal point of the composition, is quite freely treated.

Remember, though, that, if you are using water to blend the colors, it is often easier to simplify the image into areas of pure unmixed color. This is because a clogged, overworked surface will result if colored pencils are used one on top of the other indefinitely. For this reason, the artist has kept the figure simple and direct, relying on single colors and the dramatic contrast of light and shade on the form, rather than attempting to build up complex layers of color. Thus, the shaded side of the woman, her back, is mainly blocked in with black. The front of the woman, her front profile, has been left as white paper. Between these two extremes, the colors used are minimal – just a few flesh tones and the bright red of the dress.

WATERCOLOR PALETTE
A set of 24 watercolor pencils
SUPPORT
Smooth illustration board
356 × 508mm (14 × 20in)

1. BLOCKING IN THE DRESS
Block in the shadows of the dress in black, the lighter dress areas in red, and the flesh tones in light pink. Use the pencils in exactly the same way as you would work with ordinary, colored ones, building up the tones in layers of cross-hatched strokes.

2. THE FACE
Use a mid brown for the facial shadows, blending these into the lighter areas with an eraser to achieve a smooth transition between the light and dark planes.

3. BUILDING UP
Continue building up the planes, using several layers of light, regular strokes for the dark tones – this is better than trying to establish these tones by pressing heavily on the pencils. Not only does the lighter rendering look more effective, but the colors are also easier to control when used in this way.

4. HIGHLIGHT
When blocking in the background behind the figure, use the white paper to represent the highlight along your model's profile. Use a sharp pencil to ensure a crisp shape.

5. INTERIOR TONES
Use a ruler for the straight lines of the window frame, rendering these with neat, regular strokes. Working in loose strokes, block in the interior tones – the wall underneath the window and the shadow behind the figure.

6. THE VIEW
Loosely sketch in the view as seen through the window, blocking in the tones and the approximate shapes of the bridge, trees and river.

7. BLENDING CONTOURS
Now, using a sable brush and clean water, start to blend the colors of the scene framed by the window.

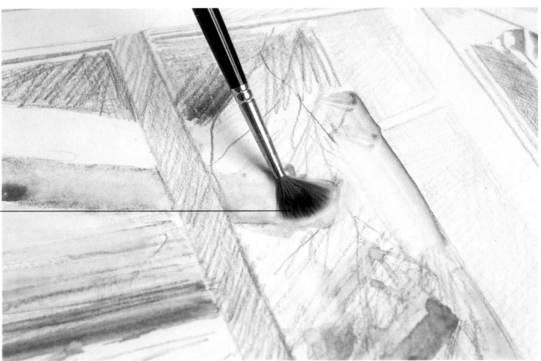

8. WASHES AND BLOBS
Instead of looking for detail, aim to create loose washes and blots of color – an effect similar to that of conventional watercolor painting.

9. THE FINISHED PICTURE
The completed picture shows how two techniques – the loose pencil hatching and the smoother blended tones – can be used in a creative and spontaneous way to enhance the subject. By blending the outdoor colors, the artist has created a picture within a picture, contrasting the interior of the room with the scene outside it.

MIXED MEDIA

WATERCOLOR CAN BE – and has been – combined with almost every other medium, including oil paint. Because watercolor can be applied in thin, flat washes, you can begin by blocking in the subject with pale areas of paint. The color dries without affecting the texture, or the surface of the paper. This means that you can then work on the dried surface with a great variety of drawing materials – pen and ink, charcoal, pencils, Magic Marker, pastel, and many others – singly or in combination.

You can also exploit the fact that watercolor does not mix with wax or oil. If you apply wax crayon, oil pastel, turpentine or thin oil paint to an area of the paper, it will resist the watercolor, and the area covered will remain intact – part of the color and texture of the picture.

Working with mixed media allows the artist scope for creativity and experimentation. As you try out different materials, you will become more familiar with their particular qualities, and with the way they react in combination. As your skill increases, you will be able to experiment with increasing confidence and success; for, more than any other area of watercolor, this is a field where personal taste and originality play an important role.

WATERCOLOR ON OIL PASTEL
1. Apply the oil pastel.

2. Lightly wash the color over the pastel. Try not to scrub the pastel with your brush.

3. The oil pastel resists the paint, and its color shows through the wash.

GOUACHE, CHARCOAL AND OIL PASTEL

1. Apply an initial layer of color, using gouache.

3. You can also draw on the gouache with charcoal.

2. Work over the gouache with oil pastel.

4. Next, add more watercolor, or gouache. The oil pastel resists the paint, but the charcoal mixes, unless it has been protected with fixative.

5. Continue to experiment by adding more broken color. Other materials, such as ink, pencil, and chalk can be introduced to create different effects.

6. The varied materials have combined to produce a result where each is still visible; thus contributing to the final effect.

CORN ON THE COB

THIS IS A BOLD experiment with a simple subject and a plain, rather severe style of composition, which could easily have failed, but is enlivened by the use of mixed media.

The picture is basically a watercolor, but the artist used white gouache for the light tones, highlights and some of the linear detail, all of which were added in the later stages. The aim from the start was to achieve a stark, graphic simplicity. The shadows were deliberately painted in a rather flat and dull gray, so that initially they had no more than a compositional role, the straight lines being broken by the organic shape of the stalk of corn. To offset the flatness, the artist worked vigorously into the lines of shadow with a loosely scribbled cross-hatching. This was particularly emphasized in the darker shadows thrown by the corn.

Colored and graphite pencils were used for the cross-hatching and other parts of the picture, which contributed to the variety of textures. Both types of pencil adhere very well to a matt-painted surface, though the disadvantage is that you cannot easily rub out the marks. Unless you are very experienced, it is best to use pencils in areas where spontaneity will work well, rather than for the more definitive parts of a picture. In any case, it is more effective if you restrict the textured part of a picture to selected areas. Should you overdo this process, the image can look bitty.

WATERCOLOR PALETTE	
Yellow Ochre	Raw Umber
Cadmium Yellow	Sap Green
Payne's Gray	Ivory Black
Lemon Yellow	
Gouache	
Titanium White	
SUPPORT	
Ivorex Card	
381 × 508mm (15 × 20in)	

1. THE MAIN SHAPES
Working without a preliminary drawing, wash in the main shapes of the corn, positioning the subject fairly centrally and leaving plenty of space around it. Use sap green for the leaves and cadmium yellow with yellow ochre for the corn.

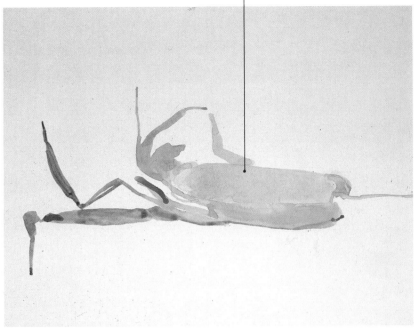

2. BUILDING UP
Using deeper versions of the initial washes, work into the corn, building up and strengthening the basic colors. Refer constantly to the subject, using dark tones to suggest the form and shape of the cob.

3. THE TABLETOP
Mix a weak wash of yellow ochre plus a little raw umber to block in the first warm tones of the tabletop. When this has dried, use Payne's gray to depict the strong criss-cross shadows and to pick out the shadows under the leaves.

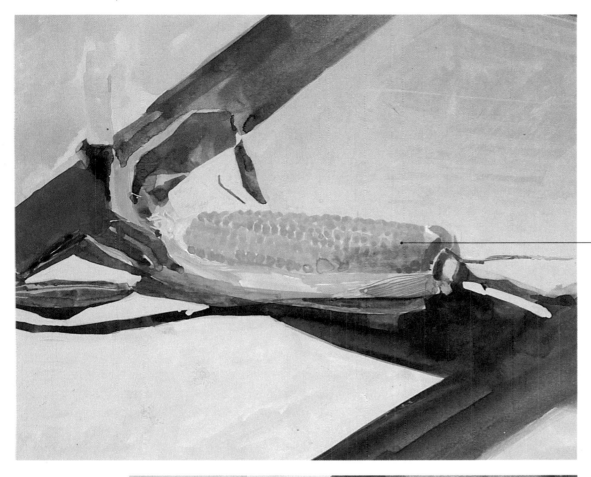

4. DEVELOPING TEXTURE
Working with the tip of a No. 3 brush, start to develop the texture and detail on the corn. Paint the striped leaves with sap green mixed with a touch of ivory black; add the dark patches on the corn with raw umber, and suggest the surface texture with regular brushstrokes of cadmium yellow and raw umber.

5. THE FOLIAGE
Using the same brush, paint the feathery parts of the foliage in fine lines of diluted black and white. Look closely at the subject and simplify what you see, taking care to make the painted version as subtle as it is in real life. Clumsily painted lines will dominate and spoil the work.

6. THE SEED SHAPES
Use lemon mixed with white gouache to clarify the tiny seed shapes on the corn, and then dot in small dark shadow tones of raw umber. When these are dry, add a sharp white highlight to each one, defining the surface texture of the cob.

7. LEAF LINES
Use thin white gouache to paint light lines on the leaves – this brings out the brittle-looking ridges of the foliage.

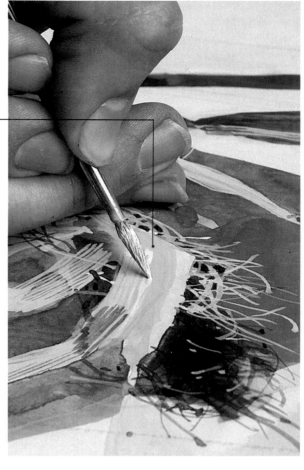

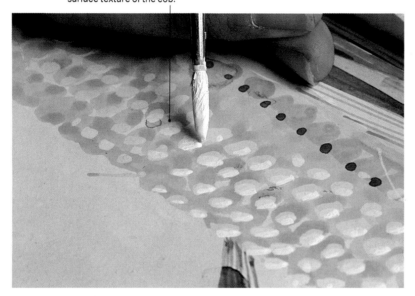

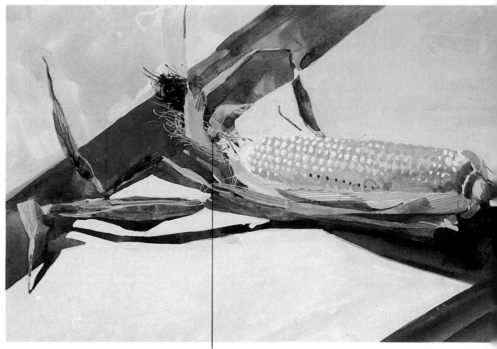

8. SHADOW SPOTS
Scribble more deep shadow spots into the corn with a graphite drawing pencil. The matt paint surface takes the pencil well, with the lightest scribbled marks showing up as quite dark shapes.

9. LINEAR DETAILS
Use colored pencils to draw in linear details elsewhere. Here, dark green and dark gray are used to develop the leaf patterns, with some light gray on the highlights.

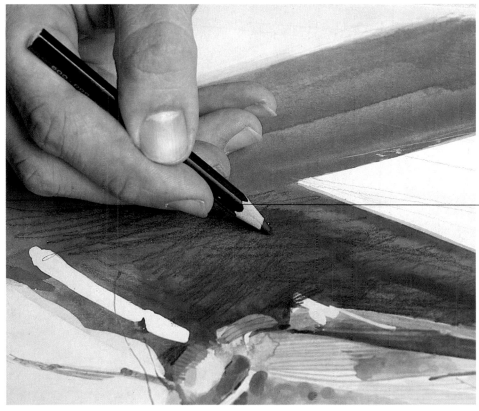

10. DARKENING THE SHADOWS
Work into the shadows with a black pencil, breaking up the flat gray shapes into areas of rich, dark texture. Enliven the painted surface with bold scribbled cross-hatching strokes, also using them to darken the shadows around the corn.

11. THE FINISHED PAINTING
The characteristics of the corn have been captured exactly in watercolor and white gouache, with some textural pencil work in the final stages. The use of white gouache enabled the artist to build up the pale tones and highlights and to sculpt the seeded surface by dabbing bright white over pitted pencil shadows.

SIMPLE TECHNIQUES

IF YOU FIND A particular subject complicated or difficult, remember that sometimes there is a simple way of tackling it. One point to bear in mind is that, although most artists paint what they see, parts of their pictures are often rendered according to a standard formula, which they may well have worked out over the years.

There is nothing wrong with reverting to a well-tried technique – indeed, such techniques can often be adapted to help you depict a specific problem subject. Beginners, for instance, often find water, skies and trees daunting; if, however, you study the work of professional artists – and that of great masters of the past – you will frequently find that they, too, have been confronted with the same problems and have developed their own, often simplified, ways of coping with them.

WINTER TREES

IT IS IMPORTANT to look at trees in the same way that the figure painter looks at the human form. When painting the figure, an artist must bear in mind the bones and muscles which dictate the visible shapes and forms. Trees, too, have skeletons – underlying structures which dictate the shape and form of the whole – even though these may be hidden by thick foliage. To paint trees successfully, you must always be aware of this structure and the forms within it.

Look at trees during the winter months, when you can see clearly the growth pattern of the trunk, branches and twigs. When drawing and painting trees, start with the main trunk and the larger branches, working outwards towards the smaller twigs, as the artist has done in this project. Pay particular attention to the shape of the spaces between the branches and twigs: these will help you to establish the positive shapes – the branches themselves.

1. BASIC SHAPE
Start with the trunk and main branches, looking carefully at the way in which the branches radiate from the main trunk, and at the shapes of the spaces created between these branches. Use a light wash – here, the artist worked in black and raw umber – with a darker tone of the same color to suggest the shadows on the rounded forms.

2. SMALLER BRANCHES
Draw the smaller branches with the tip of the brush, working outwards from the main forms.

WATERCOLOR PALETTE	
Black	Raw Umber
SUPPORT	
Stretched cartridge paper 254 × 356mm (10 × 14in)	

3. SHADOWS
Introduce bold, black shadows to the trunk and main branches – this helps to create a sense of volume and solidity.

4. FOREGROUND BRANCHES
You can also give a feeling of space to the tree by darkening some of the foreground branches, so causing them to stand out from the main tree shape.

5. FINISHED TREE
There is no secret formula for painting trees; however, because every tree, whatever the type, has a similar structure, you can always start with this basic approach. At the same time, every tree is different, and must be carefully studied and analyzed if it is to be painted successfully.

SUMMER TREES

ONE OF THE tricks to remember when painting trees in the distance is to avoid the temptation to paint details that you know to be there, even if you cannot actually see them. What you must try to do is to capture the specific shape and structure of the trees, which is evident even from a distance.

Remember, too, that there is no "correct" way to paint trees; various techniques can be used, as this picture demonstrates. You can paint them with a brush, working from light to dark and either building up the leaves as small dabs of color, or treating the foliage more broadly as a single mass. Alternatively, you can use a sponge – the rounded end of a synthetic sponge is perfect for the umbrella-shaped branches of certain trees

WATERCOLOR PALETTE

Cobalt Blue	Sap Green
Lemon Yellow	Sepia
Payne's Gray	

SUPPORT

Bockingford paper, stretched
356 × 533mm (14 × 21in)

1. THE SKY
Working on stretched paper, block in the sky in diluted cobalt blue with a No. 18 wash brush. Leave white gaps to represent the clouds and make the color fainter towards the horizon by spreading the paint with water.

2. BRANCHES AND FOLIAGE
Mix a thin wash of sap green, lemon yellow and a little sepia for the trees in a shallow mixing dish or saucer. Using the rounded end of a synthetic sponge, dab in the shapes of the branches and foliage.

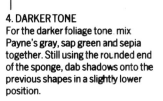

3. ESTABLISHING SHAPES
Continue applying this initial light tone with the sponge until all the main tree shapes are well established.

4. DARKER TONE
For the darker foliage tone mix Payne's gray, sap green and sepia together. Still using the rounded end of the sponge, dab shadows onto the previous shapes in a slightly lower position.

5. SPONGING PRECAUTION
Do not overdo the sponging – too much will flatten the texture and spoil the effect. As here, a few lively marks are sufficient to indicate the form of the leafy branches.

6. TWIGS AND BRANCHES
Paint in the twigs and branches with
the tip of a round sable brush, using
a thin solution of Payne's gray.

7. THE CONIFERS
Mix a thin wash of Payne's gray and
sap green for the conifers, painting
these initially as flat shapes.

8. DEVELOPING THE CONIFERS
Use the edge of a flat wash brush to develop the conifers further, applying bold vertical marks in a deeper mix of Payne's gray and sap green

9. DARKENING THE WHOLE
Take this dark tone into the rest of the composition. Work quickly, allowing the loose blobs of color and the brushmarks to describe the foliage.

10. FINISHING TOUCHES
Finally, block in the foreground in Payne's gray, sap green, adding touches of lemon to this to indicate the sunlit areas between the trees.

CHOPPY WAVES

THIS SUBJECT, the frothy, rough effect of choppy waves, is a favorite of the artist, who has developed his own particular approach to the problem of capturing the movement of the water. He starts by using horizontal brush-strokes to indicate reflective areas of the water, developing on this slightly with added darker color.

The key element here is the white gouache, which is first rolled thickly on with the brush to suggest the texture of the froth or foam. Thinner white gouache is then spattered along the top of the foreground waves to create a convincing imitation of spray.

WATERCOLOR PALETTE	
Sap Green	Payne's Gray
Ceruleum	
Gouache	
Titanium White	
SUPPORT	
Daler watercolor board 356 × 406mm (14 × 16in)	

1. BETWEEN THE WAVES
Mix a weak solution of sap green and Payne's gray and apply this with a wash brush in broad triangular streaks to represent the dark areas of water between the waves.

2. SURFACE RIPPLES
After the first wash has dried, work into the same areas with a deeper version of the same color, plus a little ceruleum. Apply the new color in horizontal strokes to indicate the shadows of the surface ripples. The ripples in the foreground should be choppier and more pronounced than those in the distance.

30

3. USE OF GOUACHE
Roll thick white gouache across the white areas of paper to create the frothy texture of the waves.

4. SPATTERING
Mix some white gouache to a runny consistency and spatter the crests of the waves with a small decorator's brush, to achieve the impression of foam.

5. FINISHING TOUCHES
Finally, change to a smaller brush and spot in tiny white flecks to represent patches of froth on the water.

WATERFALL

A SHALLOW WATERFALL tumbles into a pool surrounded by rocks and grass – the artist has captured the movement through the ripples on the surface of the water, which radiate outwards from where the waterfall flows into the pool. The ripples are simply described in terms of light and shade, while the addition of a little spattering as an extra touch brings the waterfall to life.

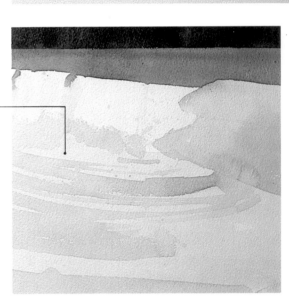

1. POOL AND GRASS
Loosely splash a pale mixture of sap green and indigo across the pool area with a wash brush. Paint the grass with a fairly deep sap green and then leave the paint to dry.

2. FOLIAGE AND ROCKS
Mix a slightly darker solution of cobalt blue and ivory black, and wash in the swirling surface of the pool, leaving the light ripple shapes unpainted. Block in the dark foliage across the top of the composition in sap green mixed with ivory black, and paint the rocks in a very pale wash of ivory black and yellow ochre.

3. CREATING THE RIPPLES
When the water area is dry, work into it with a deeper wash of sap green, cobalt blue and a little black. Again, leave most of the ripple shapes untouched, and create new ones by leaving more swirling shapes unpainted. Use ivory black for the shaded undersides of the rocks, dragging the color into the water to represent reflections.

WATERCOLOR PALETTE	
Sap Green	Indigo
Cobalt Blue	Ivory Black
Yellow Ochre	
SUPPORT	
Stretched cartridge paper 305 × 381mm (12 × 15in)	

31

4. RIPPLE SHADOWS
Using a smaller brush, such as a No. 4 sable, paint in the shadows of the ripples. Use black, sap green and cobalt blue for this, picking out the underside of the ripple shapes, and adding new smaller ripples around those already depicted around the waterfall.

5. FINISHING TOUCHES
Still using the shadow color, paint in the dark shaded ridge along the bottom of the waterfall in jagged, vertical brushstrokes. Complete the painting by shaking a few flecks of color from the brush across the lighter, top edge of the waterfall to break up the large area of reflection and to give the impression of spray.

SWIMMING POOL

THE PROBLEM WITH painting this swimming pool was to capture the quickly-changing shapes on the surface of the water. The artist could have worked from a photograph or, as here, by carefully studying the characteristic shapes of the water in life and then aiming deliberately to give an artistic, rather than a totally realistic, impression in the actual painting.

The moving surface was also suggested by the distortions of the figure under water and the broken lines of reflection in the pool itself.

1. THE FIRST TONES
Start by making a light outline sketch of the figure with an H pencil. Then, with a small sable brush, such as a No. 2, block in the lighter figure tones with a pale wash of alizarin crimson and cadmium yellow. Allow to dry before painting in the second lightest tone in a mixture of sepia and brown madder alizarin. Carefully observing the shape of the figure through the distorting ripples of the water, mix a little ultramarine with the flesh tone and paint in the shadow tones of the parts of the figure that are underwater.

2. SHADOWS AND HAIR
Mix a deeper version of the cool shadow tone, using these to develop the dark underwater shadows and to block in the hair.

WATERCOLOR PALETTE	
Alizarin Crimson	Cadmium Yellow
Brown Madder Alizarin	Sepia
Ultramarine Blue	Black
Scarlet Lake	Manganese Blue

SUPPORT
Bockingford paper, stretched
381 × 508mm (15 × 20in)

3. DARKS AND WARMS
Look for the deepest shadow tones on the subject, and block these in with a mixture of black and ultramarine. Add flecks of contrasting warm tone to the figure in brown madder alizarin mixed with scarlet lake. Allow to dry.

4. LIGHT WATER TONES
Paint in the lightest water tone with a very diluted solution of manganese blue and using a wash brush. Leave flecks of white paper showing to represent the highlights. Change to a smaller brush to take the color up to the edge of the figure. Allow the water color to dry.

5. MEDIUM TONE
Pick out the medium-toned shapes of the water with a deeper wash of manganese blue and using a No. 4 brush.

6. REFLECTIONS
Work across the water surface, applying the blue in loose, swirling strokes, trying to capture the character of the shapes and reflections. Add a little cadmium yellow to the blue as you move towards the bottom of the picture – this will give the water a greenish glow.

7. BLOCKING IN
Once the paint has dried, work over the water area with a mixture of ultramarine and manganese blue, blocking in the darkest reflections with this deep water tone.

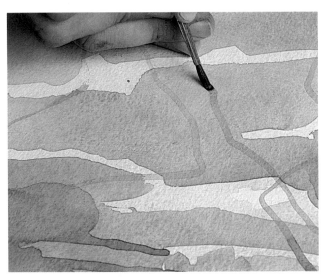

8. LINEAR REFLECTIONS
Use a wash brush for the large areas, and a No. 2 sable for the linear reflections that zig-zag vertically across the water.

9. MULTIPLE TONES
A close-up of the water shows how simple the technique actually is to follow. The artist has used three tones of blue, allowing the paint to dry in between the various layers. Color was built up from light to dark, so creating the impression of moving light and reflections on the surface of the water.

GLOSSARY

ABSTRACT ART Art which does not depend upon a realistic approach to the subject matter to express form, color and shape.

ACRYLIC PAINT Paint in which the pigment is bound with a synthetic resin. Developed in the 1920s and 1930s, acrylics do not fade and are resistant to atmospheric and weather conditions. Acrylics are diluted with water, but, once dry, they become insoluble. The paint can be used thickly like oils, or thinly to obtain an effect similar to that of watercolor painting.

ADDITIVE MIXING When the wavelengths of the light primaries – red, green and blue – are combined, the result is white. This is known as "additive mixing".

AERIAL PERSPECTIVE Distance and space are represented in painting by the way the artist depicts the air, or atmosphere. As objects recede into the distance they look fainter because they are seen through a haze of atmospheric particles.

ALCOHOL Spirit used to speed up the drying process of paint.

ASPECTIVE An unnaturalistic style of representation practised in ancient Egypt and found in many naive paintings today. Figures and objects are usually depicted in profile or with a full frontal view; scenes and landscapes contain no indication of perspective or scale.

BINDER A medium which is mixed with pigment to make paint. The traditional binder used in watercolor paints is gum arabic.

BISTER A brownish pigment, traditionally made from soot or charred wood. In the 18th century bister was used mainly as a wash – Rembrandt's pen and wash drawings are a good example of this.

BODY COLOR Opaque paint, such as gouache, which has the "hiding" or "covering" capacity to obliterate underlying color. White body color is sometimes mixed with pure watercolor to make the paint less transparent.

BLOCKING IN Roughly filling in the main shapes and forms of the overall composition before developing specific areas or adding detail.

BRIGHT A short-bristled brush with a squared end.

CALLIGRAPHIC A term used to describe the artist's technique. "Calligraphic" brushwork generally means free, loose strokes which are used to produce a visual rhythm, similar to that of handwriting.

CARTOON A full-scale drawing, or design, on paper, usually done for a painting, mural or other finished work. The design is transferred onto the final support either by pricking the outline with pins, or by chalking the back of the cartoon and retracing the lines to reproduce a faint, chalky impression of the subject.

CLASSICAL Conforming to the tastes and models of ancient Greece and Rome. In the 18th century there was enormous interest in learning from the antiquities, hence the term "Neoclassical".

COMPLEMENTARY COLOR Each of the primaries – red, blue and yellow – has an opposite, or complementary, color created by mixing the remaining two primaries: for example, the complementary color of red is green, which is a mixture of blue and yellow.

COMPOSITION Arranging or putting together the different elements of a subject to create a satisfying whole. The word is also sometimes used to describe a work of art, usually of a scene, or a group of objects or people.

COOL COLOR Color which is predominantly blue, green or violet.

CROSS-HATCHING Shading created by layers of overlapping parallel lines. The term usually applies to drawing, but cross-hatching is occasionally done in painting, especially tempera.

CUBISM A modern art movement started in Paris in the early 20th century by Picasso and Braque. The Cubists sought to analyze the structure, space and color of the subject and to interpret these instead of making a purely representational painting. Cubism is generally regarded as being the forerunner of all abstract art.

DARK OVER LIGHT Because pure watercolor is transparent, the colors must be applied using the lightest tones first – hence "dark over light". The expression "light to dark" means the same thing.

DRYBRUSH A technique in which the moisture is squeezed from the brush before being loaded with fairly thick or undiluted paint. This is then dragged across the surface of the paper to create areas of broken color and texture.

EARTH COLORS Colors made from those pigments which come from the metal oxides. These include the siennas, umbers and ochers

ENGRAVING Print taken from a metal plate on which a design or drawing has been gouged out with acid. The rest of the surface of the plate is protected from the acid by a coat of ground – a substance made from asphalt, beeswax, gum-mastic and pitch.

FERRULE The metal part of a paintbrush which holds the bristles in place.

FIGURATIVE A term used to describe works of art in which the subject is usually depicted as a recognizable form.

FILBERT A paintbrush which has flattened bristles and a tapered end.

FLAT A paintbrush which has short, flattened bristles.

FRESCO Wall-painting done on plaster in a medium similar to watercolor.

FRESCO BUONO "True" fresco, in which color is applied while the plaster is wet. The technique, practised in Italy since the 13th century, is one of the most permanent forms of painting known.

FRESCO SECCO Less enduring than fresco buono, fresco secco is color painted onto dry plaster.

FUGITIVE COLOR A pigment which fades quickly, or is otherwise impermanent.

FUTURISM A modern Italian art movement dating from 1909 which rejected the stagnant, predictable art of the time, turning instead to the contemporary themes of speed, machines and violence for its inspiration.

GLYCERINE A liquid obtained from the fat and oil of vegetables or animals and used in the manufacture of watercolors.

GOUACHE An opaque type of watercolor, sometimes referred to as "body color".

GRAIN The texture of paper or card. This may be fine or coarse, and is an important factor in creating paint effects.

GRAPHITE A type of carbon also known as "black lead" used in the manufacture of pencils. The carbon is compressed with clay for pencil making,

and is also available in sticks and powder form.

GUM ARABIC Water soluble gum from the acacia tree which is used as a binder in watercolor and gouache paints. Gum arabic can also be used to enhance the texture and color of paints.

GYPSUM The mineral from which plaster of Paris is made. One of the earliest white pigments used in painting.

HATCHING Shading by means of regular parallel lines. Mainly a drawing technique, hatching is occasionally used by painters, especially those working in tempera.

HERBAL A book containing the names, and usually the illustrations, of herbs and plants.

HIGH RENAISSANCE The later period of the Italian Renaissance, dating from about 1500 to 1527, which includes the works of Leonardo da Vinci and the earlier works of Michelangelo.

IMPRESSIONISM One of the most important movements in contemporary art. Impressionism was born in Paris in 1874 and its exponents – including Monet, Sisley, Renoir and Pissarro – were concerned chiefly with the effects of light and color rather than line and structure. They often used bright, broken color to achieve the shimmering effects of nature.

KELMSCOTT PRESS A printing press started by William Morris in 1890, for which he designed the type faces and the decorations.

LINEAR PERSPECTIVE Based on the rule that receding parallel lines on the same plane converge at a point on the horizon – the vanishing point. The system is used by artists to create accurate spatial distance in a picture.

LOCAL COLOR The color of an object when it has not been modified by light, shadow or atmosphere.

MANNERISM A style of painting in Italy, dating from about 1520-1600, which was based to a large extent on the influence of Michelangelo. It is characterized by elongated, sinuous figures and theatrical gestures.

MASKING The process of protecting the support, or an area of color, when another color is applied.

MASKING FLUID A liquid rubber solution which is painted onto the support to mask certain areas from subsequent paint. Color can be applied over the areas masked by the fluid. The dried mask is eventually rubbed off with an eraser or finger.

MATT KNIFE Cutting tool with a removable blade. The matt knife was originally used for surgical purposes, but is widely employed by artists, designers and craftspeople.

MEZZOTINT A finely grained printing method popular in the 18th century which enabled the engraver to obtain precise tones. It has largely been replaced by photographic reproduction methods.

MEDIUM The material in which a painting or drawing is executed – watercolor, oils, colored pencil, etc. The term is also used to describe the various additives which can be mixed with the paint by the artist in order to change the effect or the property of the material.

MIXED MEDIA A work of art created from a variety of media. The combination can be traditional, such as watercolor and ink, or the mixture can be more experimental. Contemporary works often contain a variety of materials.

MONOCHROME A drawing or painting done in one color.

MOP A watercolor brush with a full, round head of bristles useful for large areas of color and washes.

NEOCLASSICAL An 18th century movement whose aims were to recreate the standards and styles of Greece and Rome.

"NOT" A term used to describe paper manufactured by being cold-pressed rather than hot-pressed (the paper is not hot-pressed, hence the origin of the expression "not" paper.

OLD STONE AGE The paleolithic period, or first part of the Stone Age, when tools and implements were stones and flints chipped into various shapes.

OPACITY When referring to paint, this term means the "covering" or "hiding" ability of a paint, or color, to obliterate the underlying color.

PALETTE A tray, board, or mixing dish used for mixing and thinning paints. The term is also used to describe a selection of colors as used by a particular artist, or in a specific picture.

PARCHMENT Support for writing or painting on, made from animal skin, usually sheep or goat.

PIGMENT Coloring substances obtained from mineral, animal or vegetable sources. The same pigments are used to make all types of paint.

POINTILLISM A painting technique based on the optical mixing of colors – allowing the colors to mix in the viewer's eye rather than pre-mixing them on the palette: for example, an area of green might be largely built up with tiny dots of yellows and blues, and modified with a few other colors.

POSTER COLOR An opaque type of watercolour. Poster color is similar to gouache, but is a cruder product and is generally available in a fairly limited range of colors.

PRE-RAPHAELITE BROTHERHOOD A 19th century English movement which looked to the art of 14th and 15th century Italy for its inspiration. The artists used bright colors, sharp detail, and featured mythology and symbolism in much of their work.

PRIMARY COLOR Artists' primary colors are red, yellow and blue. Theoretically, all other colors can be made from the three primaries, although in practise this is not the case.

PURE COLOR The primary colors – red, yellow and blue – and any mix of two of them, are referred to as "pure".

RENAISSANCE Artistic and cultural revival of classical ideals which took place in Europe, particularly Italy, from the 14th to the 16th centuries.

RESIST Technique involving two materials which do not mix: for example wax crayon or oil paint used under watercolor will repel, or resist, the paint to produce a particular effect.

RIGGER A soft brush with long, tapering bristles, used mainly by calligraphers and sign-writers, but also employed by painters to produce flowing, undulating lines.

ROMANTIC MOVEMENT An 18th century art movement which was concerned primarily with the expression and emphasis of idealized human emotion.

ROUND Standard brush type with bristles which are held in a circular ferrule.

SABLE Kolinsky, or Siberian weasel. The hairs from the tail of this small rodent are used for making superior paintbrushes.

SATURATION Term used to describe the strength or intensity of a color.

SCALPEL Cutting tool with a removable blade. The scalpel was originally used for surgical purposes, but is widely employed by artists, designers and craftspeople.

SECONDARY COLOR Color mixed from two of the primary colours. Orange, green and violet are the secondary colors in painting.

SEPIA Brownish pigment, traditionally obtained from the ink of the cuttlefish.

SGRAFFITO Scratching or scoring technique, usually done with a sharp instrument, to lift the color in order to reveal the white paper underneath.

SIZE Glue obtained from animal skin and used for sealing canvas and paper.

SKETCH A rapid drawing aimed at capturing the essential elements of a subject. A sketch is often made to work out a particular aspect of the subject prior to painting it, or to be used as reference for a painting to be done at a later date.

SPATTERING Texturing technique done by shaking a loaded brush onto the picture, or by flicking color from the brush with the thumb or finger.

STENCIL Card, or other stiff material, with a pattern or motif cut out of it. The stencil is laid on the support and the paint dabbed over the cut out areas to reproduce the design.

STIPPLE Texture created by dabbing color with a special brush. A stippling brush has a short stiff head of bristles cut squarely to form a flat end when the brush is used in an upright position.

SUBTRACTIVE MIXING Mixing of the artists' primaries – red, yellow and blue – to create secondary and tertiary colors. When these three are mixed in equal quantities the result is dark gray.

SUPPORT Paper, canvas, board, or other surface on which to paint or draw.

TEMPERA Paint made from pigment, an emulsion of oil, and water. Tempera popularly means egg tempera in which the emulsion used is egg yolk.

TERTIARY COLORS Colors which are the result of a primary color mixed with an equal amount of a secondary color.

THUMBNAIL SKETCH Tiny line or colour sketches done to help the artist

make decisions about composition, color, etc, before embarking on a full-scale work.

TONE Light and dark values are referred to as tones. Every local color has a tone – an equivalent gray. Gradations of tone are also created by the effect of light and shade on a three-dimensional object.

TOPOGRAPHY Detailed, descriptive drawing aimed at showing the specific features of a scene. The object of a topographical drawing is to convey information about the subject rather than to express a personal interpretation of it.

VANISHING POINT The theoretical point at which converging parallel lines meet when constructing linear perspective.

VARNISH Transparent, resinous coat applied to the finished painting to protect the surface.

VORTICISM English art movement similar to Cubism, formed by the painter and writer, Wyndham Lewis.

WARM COLOR Reds, oranges and yellows are the warm colors.

WASH Diluted color applied thinly to the support. A wash can be graded from light to dark, or can be laid in two or more colors. The object of a wash is usually to obtain an area of transparent color in the early stages of a painting.

WATERCOLOR Waterbased paint made from pigment suspended in gum arabic. Unlike most other paints, watercolor is transparent and must be worked by laying the lightest tones first.

WAX RESIST Resist technique based on the fact that wax repels water; candles, wax crayons, or any other waxy substance can be used.

WET ON DRY Applying paint to a color which has been allowed to dry thoroughly, or to a dry support, in order to achieve crisp shapes and controlled brushstrokes.

WET ON WET Applying paint to a color while it is still wet, or to a dampened support, in order to achieve soft forms and bleeding colors.

INDEX

INDEX

ACKNOWLEDGMENTS

THE PAUL PRESS LTD would like to thank all those who have helped with this book. We would especially like to thank George Short for his patience and journalistic expertise, Ian Sidaway and Ian Howes for all their hard work and long hours, and Daler-Rowney for their help and generosity in providing materials for the demonstrations and studio photography.

The Paul Press Ltd would also like to thank the following organizations to whom copyright in the photographs noted belongs:

11 The Bridgeman Art Library; 12 Michael Holford; 13 The British Library; 14-15 The Bridgeman Art Library; 17,18 reproduced by courtesy of the Trustees of the British Museum; 19 Michael Holford; 21 Graphische Sammlung Albertina, Vienna; 23 The Bridgeman Art Library; 25 Photo Vatican Museums; 27,29 reproduced by courtesy of the Trustees of the British Museum; 31,33 by courtesy of the Board of Trustees of the Victoria and Albert Museum; 34 National Portrait Gallery, London; 35 by courtesy of the Board of Trustees of the Victoria and Albert Museum; 37 reproduced by courtesy of the Trustees of the British Museum; 39 The Bridgeman Art Library; 43 Tate Gallery, London; 44 reproduced by courtesy of the Trustees of the British Museum; 45 Bridgeman Art Library; 47 Bridgeman Art Library; 49 reproduced by courtesy of the Trustees of the British Museum; 50 The Bridgeman Art Library; 51 reproduced by courtesy of the Trustees of the British Museum; 53 The Bridgeman Art Library; 54, 55 National Museum of Wales; 57 Sterling and Francine Clark Institute, Williamstown, Mass; 58 Nationalmuseum, Stockholm; 61 The Metropolitan Museum of Art, Fletcher Fund, 1925 (25.97.1); 62 Hunterian Art Gallery, University of Glasgow, Birnie Philip Gift; 63 Worcester Art Museum, Worcester, MA; 64 Gift of Eleanor Conway Sawyer, Dickinson College, Carlisle, PA; 65 The Bridgeman Art Library; 67 Courtauld Institute Galleries, London (Courtauld Collection); 68 The Imperial War Museum; 69 Solomon R. Guggenheim Museum, New York; Photo: David Heald (c ADAGP 1986); 70 The Justin K. Thannhauser Collection, Solomon R. Guggenheim Museum, New York; Photo: David Heald (c DACS 1986); 71 by courtesy of the Board of Trustees of the Victoria and Albert Museum; 85, 86 (top) Daler-Rowney